By William Joyce:

First Born of an Ass (novel)
The Recorder of Births and Deaths (stories)
For Women Who Moan (poems)
Listen America, You Don't Even Own Your Name
(poems)

Miller, Bukowski & Their Enemies

essays
on
contemporary
culture

**William
Joyce**

Avisson Press, Inc.
Greensboro

Copyright © 1996 by William Joyce
All rights reserved

Published by:
Avisson Press, Inc.
P.O. Box 38816
Greensboro, North Carolina 27438 USA

ISBN 1-888105-11-9
LCCN 96-85582
First Edition
Manufactured in the United States of America

Dedication

For Jack Shafer, the rare editor with balls.

Acknowledgments

"Miller Time" first appeared in *City Paper* (Washington, D.C.) as an extended essay/review prompted by the book *The Happiest Man Alive: A Biography of Henry Miller*, by Mary V. Dearborn. "Kiss Me, I'm Still Alive" also first appeared in *City Paper*, as did "His Own Best Friend," prompted by the book *Hank: The Life of Charles Bukowski*, by Neeli Cherkovski.

"Masturbation in the Strophe Factory" is a compendium of four essays. The first, carrying that same title, appeared in *Cedar Rock*; the second, "The Present State of American Poetry II," in *New York Quarterly*; the third, "The Oink from the Literary Barn" in *American Book Review*; the fourth, "How Writers Censor Themselves" in *Yokoi*.

contents

miller time:
on henry miller

Henry Miller is not a writer; he's a friend you turn to when your apartment walls close in on you and all the world begins to stink. When you're most exasperated, Miller is there with his alternately cajoling, absurd, sincere, outraged, sage-like, funny voice, ruminating and gassing in a calm way. Miller's voice always comes from the quietest corner of the bar. The rest of the occupants are slaughtering each other, offering polemical speeches, toasting their various diseases, and gouging their own thighs and arms with their fingernails in an effort to rid themselves of the itch of being truly alive. Unlike his distant cousin Celine, Miller never gets clobbered by these barroom brawlers. He gets close enough to the action to observe the lice and the whispered endearments between blows, but he never gets whacked by a piece of flying furniture. "Don't struggle; get in the flow," he advises in book after book. Much of this "flow" for Miller is in the flotsam—all sorts of deranged and eccentric characters—who are both more lively and can tell us more about life than comfortable citizens at the center. He doesn't see the same divisions the rest of us have been taught to see. Wealthy hoarders or bourgeoisie hoarders may be deplorable, but the feeling I get after 30 years of browsing through Miller is that he'd knocked aside all compartmentalization; he would sit down for a meal with anybody who was unaffected and learn from him, provided of course that the companion sprung for the meal. Miller is the greatest of all freeloaders, surpassing even that other Joyce. In return for his presence, his attentive ear, and perhaps a three-page carbon of his latest writing, all Miller asks is that his host "would open all the windows leading to his heart" (about the Greek poet George Seferiades). And so people do. That is his secret—Miller was a great listener, though he has the reputation of a monologist .

He will rage, but he is never weighed down by alienation. He is a master of language, but literature doesn't mean a damn thing to him. I feel equally at home opening a Miller book on Page 7 or Page 57. It is like picking up the thread of a conversation I had five years ago with a trusty and trusting friend. The hermetically closed systems of the modern masters such as Joyce or Kafka mean little to him; they are only further evidence of The Machine that has reduced us all to atoms bouncing off our lonely apartment walls. Like Whitman, he advises us that all we have to do is open our arms and accept the world as it is. He echoes Thoreau in telling us to get off the conveyor belt and live simply. Yet, Miller has not an ounce of Whitman's optimism about the future of the United States, and his frenetic search for money and an audience kept him on the conveyor belt more than he would like us to believe. But it is that voice of his we always come back to. Even when I realize Miller has made a wrong turn, I stick with him. I do this because Miller takes the freedom to say anything that is on his mind at any given time. There is no holding back; he never falls for the echo of his rhetoric as many other good writers do. He is a singer for sure, but it is not his melody he becomes enraptured by, only the desire to be faithful to what he has seen and felt in his heart. If this seems a small order, listen to Chekhov: "I cannot remember a single new book in which the author does not do his best from the very first line to entangle himself in all sorts of conventionalities and compromise with his conscience. Deliberateness, cautiousness, craftiness but no freedom, no courage to write as one likes, and therefore no creative art." This remark covers most of the writing of our time, as it did in Europe in the late 19th century.

Most writers are attracted to craft because it's a chance to be evasive while romanticizing themselves. Even as most lawyers come to law not to serve justice, but to cut the pie of a legally sanctioned swindle, and as teachers come to the classroom to yak non-stop, thereby advancing the cause of impotency. Part of the definition of "human being" would include the unique ability to choose the vocation for which he is least suited.

Miller had risk, he had it in abundance. This was not a matter of using shocking sexual detail, as he was often accused of. It was a huge need to make his voice grow flesh. In the first 39 years of his life, before he fully committed himself to writing, Miller felt that everything we call "progress" was separating us from ourselves as well as each other. The "literary" voice was cut off from the body, and to eliminate the body was to eliminate the soul as well. Every new building, every new invention went a step further toward slicing people into strips of potato falling from the shredder. To reconnect himself, Miller felt he had to start from scratch, disconnect all the plugs that supposedly gave him sustenance but in reality sought to make him a galley slave and slowly inch himself back to being a whole person. To read Miller then, is to listen to the first and last man on earth. Words aren't tools of the craft for him, as they are for most writers. Miller was as suspicious of them as he was of books. No, words were blasted from his liver and spleen and funny bone; they came rushing in measured torrents with lymph nodes and chunks of flesh stuck to them. There are considerable lumps in each of Miller's books where he goes off the deep end and makes no sense at all. This usually happens when he can't resist playing the new messiah and metaphysical poet wherein he trots out the stars and our relationship to the black holes in between. But always with Miller, I feel I am dealing with a man, not a code of conduct some publisher has put his stamp of approval on.

Of course there are other writers tapping away under a black firmament as if no one had ever thought to buy a typewriter before. Beckett comes to mind, with his heroes playing with their bedsores, mumbling asides to a mother who isn't there, their only company the bedpans and a few strands of aborted consciousness. Kafka is another, whispering from behind a closet door which in turn leads to another closet door that finally opens on the MLA convention in Toledo, Ohio, where K, Lucky, and Malone enter to modest applause and the pedants rise to chant, "Oh Blessed Depression, Oh Blessed Symbols." It's gotten so bad that applicants for graduate-school English departments as far away as Cameroon have to write an essay on "How My Alienation Rendered Me Comatose." Pluckier souls are relegated to teaching remedial composition and running out for cheap sherry when the visiting poet comes to town.

It is true that only the courageous ones with unique voices offer themselves up for parody (is it possible to parody Saul "Give Me an Intellectual Smooch" Bellow or John "Count the Whorls in the Bannister" Updike?), but Miller took several important steps beyond what is called "modern literature."

First, Miller said there was no reason to despair. We ought to welcome breakdown, because the moral underpinnings of society indicate no morality at all but merely a devotion to ball bearings and cotter pins. If the legacy of the 20th century is war after war, chaos, corruption, incompetence, a will toward accumulating tidy comforts, the slaughter of everything vulnerable, root it on, says Miller. Let the whole cardboard house filled with pus collapse and ooze into the streets. "Suddenly inspired by the absolute hopelessness of everything, I felt relieved, felt as though a great burden had been lifted from my shoulders," he says in *Tropic of Cancer*. As to what Miller offers to replace cars, phones, soda pop, aspirin bottles, plastic drawings, and "enriched" bread, let him speak from a Greek island in 1939. He has no money, though he has published three books, no prospects, no home or homeland:

"I would set out in the morning and look for new coves and inlets to which to swim. There was never a soul about; I was like Robinson Crusoe on the island of Tobago. For hours at a stretch I would lie in the sun doing nothing, thinking nothing. To keep the mind empty is a feat, a very healthful feat too. To be silent the whole day long, see no newspaper, hear no radio, listen to no gossip, be thoroughly and completely lazy, thoroughly and completely indifferent to the fate of the world is the finest medicine a man can give himself. The book-learning gradually dribbles away; the problems melt and dissolve; ties are gently severed; thinking, when you deign to indulge in it, becomes very primitive; the body becomes a new and wonderful instrument; you look at plants or stones with different eyes; you wonder what people are struggling to accomplish by their frenetic activities...."

Henry Miller understood it was rare to meet a man or woman who was at home on this earth. So he sought to show them the way by example and word. In a 1952 letter to Edmund Wilson, he explained that there was only one hero in his books—himself. If Miller carries the most gargantuan of egos, he also shows us how he made a mess of his life before he left for Paris in 1930. More important, he understands we are all feeling the same pressure, the same remoteness from our toes and genitals, trees and rivers, birds and other people. Yet, not only does Miller not feel alienated from other people, he assumes the world wants to hear him. This is a huge leap of faith when you consider that most people didn't want to hear him, that few publishers or agents would deal with him, that much of his best writing was banned in this country and most of Europe for 25 years, that he was so poor most of his life that he regularly had Frances Steloff, owner of the Gotham Book Mart in New York City, run ads for donations for him on her bulletin board. Miller had the rash assumption that he could convince *Time* magazine to run the same ad. And they did, free. He believed he could catch anybody's ear, and sometimes he was right. Such odd faith contributed as much as anything to grant him a fully bodied voice and convince me he's on the barstool next to me. Neither his misery nor his joys are exceptional, he infers; either can be had for the asking. Because it's impossible to put any kind of label on him, Henry Miller continues to be both a puzzle and an embarrassment to thousands of cultural arbiters in this country.

Perfect evidence of this is a recent biography of Miller from Simon & Schuster by a Ph.D. in comparative lit named Mary Dearborn. In a different way this biography, *The Happiest Man Alive,* is a reminder of the movie *Henry and June,* a film that could cure the horniest goat of any desire to copulate for six months. I say "different" because I can't figure out why a bloated corporation, a subsidiary of Paramount Communications, awarder of millions of dollars to several ex-presidents to not say anything about their criminal exploits, awarder of hundreds of thousands of dollars to one-fourth the Watergate crew to whine and weep and discover Jesus, memoirs that if taken collectively would redefine the word "illiteracy," should have the faintest interest in a writer who has never risen in popularity beyond that of a cult figure. If Henry Miller were alive today and walked into Simon & Schuster carrying a manuscript, he would be arrested on sight for vagrancy and trespassing. In fact, S&S regularly rejected Miller's books, as did a lot of other publishers. The difference is that, while other publishers occasionally took a chance on serious literary writing from newcomers, S&S waited until a couple of these writers emerged from the pack, established themselves as leading voices through two or three books, then, like a vulture smelling a nourishing carcass, swept in with its bags of entertainment loot and dangled six figures in front of head-of-the-pack's eyes.

When I telephoned Simon & Schuster to try to discover its rationale for printing this book, I was told by the book's editor, Bob Bender, that the publicity department handled all questions from reviewers.

"I don't want publicity. I need to talk to you."

"Who are you with?"

"I'm doing a piece on spec for *City Paper.*"

"Ohhh, so you're a free-lancer ...."

"Can you just tell me how Simon & Schuster came to acquire this book?"

"I have to go to a meeting; publicity will handle your questions," and presto the sweetest little voice south of Dixie Cup, Maine, came on the line: "Hi, I'm Millicent Milegate, assistant head of publicity on the Dearborn book. Can I help you?"

I tossed out the same question about acquisition and damned if I didn't get the same reply as Bender had given me: Who was I with? By this time I should have wised up; I should have said I was with *Time* magazine, the

Washington Post, or the *Boogaloo Independent.*
Because when I told her I got that same suck of air with
the extended aspiration on the "Ohhh." "Ohhh so you're
a free-lancer." By now I understood the word "free-
lancer" to signal a person who runs in the same crowd as
child abusers, shop-lifters of March of Dimes cans, and
graffiti defacers of the Statue of Liberty. Millicent,
however, did have a few minutes to offer me. No, she had
never heard of Henry Miller before she came across the
Dearborn book, which she said she was enjoying. She
was a recent graduate in English from Stony Brook.

"I'm surprised at a reputable institution like Simon &
Schuster dealing with a bum like Henry Miller," I said.

"A bum? What do you mean, a bum?"

"He panhandled."

"Right on the street?"

"Yes. On the street, in the parks, door to door,
everywhere. And worse.. ."

"Yes?"

"He piddled."

"You don't mean..."

"Yes I do. Just like a dog, anywhere he pleased."

"Ohh my. I am going to have to have a talk with my
boss. I didn't know he was that bad."

It's often assumed that the legacy of the '80s was
computer chips and greed. It was not. It was the
development of perfect and precious incisors in a
generation of young ladies. When these ladies put the
incisors into motion, it's as if each word is being minced
through a screen of soft cheese. Something as deadly as
"Saddam Hussein's Revolutionary Guard" comes out
sounding both banal and edible. Every institution has a
brigade of such ladies in its front-line trenches, their teeth
polished and straightened to consumable tuning forks,
their every word a reminder that there is nothing worth

discovering in the whole wide world.

The other partner of this unlikely marriage born out of the wedlock of a troglodyte instigator is Academia—in the form of Ms. Dearborn. She's spent some time at Columbia and won at least one "prestigious" grant. One of her previous books, *Pocahantas's Daughters: Gender and Ethnicity in American Culture,* hints at the approach she took with 20 Miller books and 88 years of his life. At first I was not alert to this approach because I read the book from the last page forward, and in the final two pages her culminating thoughts on Miller struck me as sometimes commendable, mostly sane, and only rarely dubious. For example, she says, "His rejection of the bourgeois family and everything they stood for was heroic and hard won." That is a fair enough statement. So are these: "His compassion for misfits came from the most honest and honorable source—his recognition that their struggle against the forces that threatened to engulf them (and so often did) was his struggle as well." Or: "These years of his life stand as a scathing indictment of the way American society treats its iconoclastic artists."

Any one of these valuable statements could serve as a chapter or indeed the hinges on which to hang a whole book. But not only do words like "heroic," "compassion" and "scathing indictment" not show up again, these themes are barely dealt with, and where they are it is always in the context of Miller's brutality toward various sources. My main question was this: If a 19-year old should ask me why he should read Miller, was there a paragraph or two I could show him that would offer some rationale as to why his work is important? Not finding any as I backtracked to Page 127—the last of the picture section, revealing a southern beauty named Brenda Venus draped around the birdlike neck of the 81 year-old Henry, who looks like he has a peach seed stuck in his mouth—I got desperate. I got so desperate, I bit into the core of the apple I was eating and came up with a mouthful of sour seeds. I spat them into the waste basket and made up my mind I would do like any "normal" reader; I would begin at the beginning. Surely, in the first 15 or 20 pages I would get some sense of why Dearborn devoted years of research and writing about an author whom most readers don't know (and those who have heard of him, think of him as the purveyor of offbeat smut).

I have to confess, then, I got a little excited when I spotted "What has Henry Miller to say to us now, in his centennial year?" on the third page of the preface. Dearborn's answer: "Isn't his work sexist and out of date? Because his books were banned for their sexual content he is thought to have been a freewheeling advocate of sexual expression. But 'freedom' is hardly the word to use in conjunction with a world view as sexist as Miller's. In fact, as feminist critics have pointed out..." And we're off to the races. She concludes this preface, traditionally the space allotted for discussing the worth of an author, with the following: "[H]is books can in fact reveal a great deal about sexuality and male-female relationships in our recent history...Miller's writing is difficult to evaluate; he has, for instance, received no serious academic criticism. His story from its very beginning is a story of 20th century male identity." And that's it.

In other words, Dearborn has a case on her hands, a case at times both psychopathic and neurotic. And it's not merely a matter of what she sees as his sexism. He's just as often anti-Semitic, a misogynist, a sadist, a cultist (in his devotion to astrology and various strains of Eastern kharma), a fascist, and in the most hilarious section of the book—which describes his relationship with June, his second wife and the June of the disastrous movie—he is nailed deftly and fervently to the cross of masochism. However, there is no evidence that Miller was ever cruel to animals, and that should give us some hope for his beleaguered soul .

There is no doubt Miller is an incendiary character to write about. "How is one to talk about Miller?" asks the critic and poet Karl Shapiro in his introduction to *Tropic Of Cancer*: "There are authors one cannot write a book or even a good essay about. Miller is one of those Patagonian authors who just won't fit into a book." It's not only the excruciating messiness of Miller's life that presents problems; most worthwhile writers' lives are full of chaos born of numerous false starts and wrong-headed decisions. Miller found more ways to fry himself than Colonel Sanders did chickens. But as he was fond of saying, a man's personality is formed from the ashes from which he resurrects himself. He spent the first 39 years of his life running around Manhattan and Brooklyn furiously trying to be a success in a dozen different careers including writing to order for magazines, and alternately thumbing his nose at them just to prove that he was, after all, exceptional. Miller had no likes and dislikes, just loves and hates, sometimes both for a person, a city, an ethnic group. Shapiro calls these "contradictions"; Dearborn refers to them as "ambivalence," but it is not the reconciliation of these "ambivalences" that interests her, not the finished work that Miller chose to offer the world, but the case against his repeated brutality she can make through unsold work, notes that went into future work, and hundreds of letters Miller wrote to friends and acquaintances.

In short, Dearborn fashions her argument much like a diligent district attorney. She rigorously follows the letter of the law through exhibit after exhibit but never captures the spirit of the man nor the writer Miller. On the one hand her mode of discourse is dispassionate; never once does she use the word "I," as if knowledge, indeed history, took place independent of the passions of men and beasts. In another sense she fairly gushes; a spate of adjectives spurts forth each time she discovers new evidence of a Millerism. If a Miller advocate can detach for a few hours, it is like watching a single member of a bucket brigade chase the incendiary Miller up and down the block. Now antisemitism breaks out; just about the time Dearborn gets this under control, a case of misogynism breaks out farther down the block. Then, when she has control over one end of the street, utters a sigh, and starts to give Miller his due by calling the two *Tropic* books "literature," damned if another conflagration doesn't break out from that sneaky Miller at the other end of the block and Dearborn leaves us to chase another ism. It's feverish work, and at Page 266 my book burst into flames.

Shapiro cautions against quoting Miller: "The danger is that one can find massive contradictions, unless there is some awareness of the underlying world and the cosmic attitudes of the author." I say Shapiro is only partially right; the conscientious biographer could also serve justice by viewing each sentence in the context of its paragraph and then in the context of the entire book. But once a bloodhound has caught the scent of the phallic brutality of it all, there is little one can do to stop its relentless progress. Here then, is the method of Dearborn throughout her biography: On Page 141 she says, "Miller had his revenge on Bertha Schrank [a married woman he flirted with] by including her as Tania, whose clitoris the narrator threatens to bite into—and spit out in two-franc pieces. The book *Tropic of Cancer* was shaping up as a celebration of male identity and male sexuality."

The *Tropic of Cancer* passage she refers to is on page 5 and goes like this:

"At night when I look at Boris' goatee lying on the pillow I get hysterical. O Tania, where now is that warm cunt of yours, those fat, heavy garters, those soft bulging thighs? There is a bone in my prick six inches long. I will ream out every wrinkle in your cunt, Tania, big with seed I will send you home to your Sylvester with an ache in your belly and your womb turned inside out. Your Sylvester! Yes, he knows how to build a fire, but I know how to inflame a cunt. I shoot hot bolts into you, Tania, I make your ovaries incandescent. Your Sylvester is a little jealous now? He feels something, does he? He feels the remnants of my big prick. I have set the shores a little wider. I have ironed out the wrinkles. After me you can take on stallions, bulls, rams, drakes, St. Bernards. You can stuff toads, bats, lizards, bats up your rectum. You can shit arpeggios if you like, or string a zither across your navel. I am fucking you, Tania, so you'll stay fucked. And if you are afraid of being fucked publicly I will fuck you privately. I will tear off a few hairs from your cunt and paste them on Boris' chin. I will bite into your clitoris and spit out two frank pieces . . ."

The ellipses here are not mine but Miller's, and they are important. They indicate that the whole business is a masturbation fantasy. And fantasy is exactly what gets all the male characters into trouble in *Tropic of Cancer*. They ache to find a woman, and once they find one—prostitute, girlfriend, wife—they bemoan the fact that they are trapped. The most cunt-stricken of all this sad-comic gallery is Van Norden. "But what is it you want of a woman, then?" asks the narrator-Miller.

" 'I want to be able to surrender myself to a woman,' he [Van Norden] blurts out. 'I want her to take me out of myself...' "

This is precisely the point of the whole novel. Men feel both doomed and damned by the weight of being men. They are afraid of being free; they've never broken the umbilical cord. They are in short enslaved by the idea of getting back into the womb. They do not learn, but narrator-Miller does. Toward the end of the first *Tropic* he says to himself, "Going back in a flash over the women I've known. It's like a chain which I've forged *out of my own misery* [emphasis added]. Each one bound to the other. A fear of living separate, of staying born."

In fact, the "phallic significance of things" becomes a parody of the peter in *Tropic of Cancer*. It is neither the subjugation of women nor sex itself that Miller cares about. It is the dependence on women and those accompanying fantasies that he sheds through listening to a gallery of whining men who typify the slavery to an idea (that women can be saviors) that hounds most men anywhere throughout their lives.

Dearborn never gets near the development of Miller's first book or, for that matter, any ot his books. Why should she? She's got her ax to grind, and there is plenty of fodder for it; if Miller can he taken out of context, the resolutions of his contradictions ignored, she's free to write any nonsense that sucks on the sagging tit of the latest sexual politics.

Among a cascade of totally wrong statements, she writes, "Miller wanted to banish sentiment completely" (referring to *Tropic of Cancer*). According to *Webster's New Universal Unabridged Dictionary*, sentiment is "a complex combination of feelings and opinions as a basis for action or judgment." Could a man trying "to banish sentiment completely" have written toward the end of *Tropic of Cancer*:

> Everything is packed into a second which is either consummated or not consummated. The earth is not an arid plateau of health and comfort, but a great sprawling female with velvet torso that swells and heaves as with ocean billows; she squirms beneath a diadem of sweat and anguish. Naked and sexed she rolls among the clouds in the violet light of the stars. All of her, from her generous breasts to her gleaming thighs, blazes with furious ardor. She moves among the seasons and the years with a grand whoopla that seizes the torso with paroxysmal fury, that shakes the cobwebs out of the sky; she subsides on her pivotal orbits with volcanic tremors.

This is not the obscene, trickling goo that we get in song after song, movie after movie, commercial after commercial about love. That is, love as a comfortable, harmonious prop for a dull, meager, hoarding life. Miller is not talking about Tammy meeting Blaine, complete with hand-holding and ice cream cones till death do us part. This is not the leer of the weekend sensualist who hopes a little nooky may after all lead to something important. This is not in the image of the tits-and-ass man on the page or in reality the voyeur that Dearborn claims for Miller. This is the grand celebration of all creation in the image of a woman, not earth nor woman as the passive, domesticated fodder we've all been taught to pump for ego and profit while joining a few worthwhile causes; this is awe and wonder and rejoicing at the miracle of it all. Woman is at the center of it because she gives birth; Miller here acknowledges, as most true artists have done, the woman inside himself, a woman constantly in ferment and fermentation. In short, Miller, in this first published book of his, would have us love an earth always on the edge of fruition, always about to give birth, or, for that matter, that which is always about to explode new and whole from inside us.

If you need more evidence that Miller has feeling, read the *Tropic of Cancer* passage where he defends a prostitute against his friend's charge that she is cold and mechanical and that her pimp will only waste her money:

"Remember that you're far back in the procession; remember that a whole army corps has laid siege to her, that she's been laid waste, plundered and pillaged....It's her money and her pimp. It's blood money. It's money that'll never be taken out of circulation because there's nothing in the Banque de France to redeem it with."

There is surely more sympathy here and understanding on one page than Miller gets from his definitive biographer in an entire book. Not only does *Tropic of Cancer* have "sentiment" on every page, but it's the sort of sentiment you get from a man who's bled himself of every last vestige of the conventional feelings that alternately keep us trapped within ourselves, saddled on the conveyor belt, and deranged at the thought that our lives are sailing by without much of anything happening inside us.

Mary Dearborn, for the academic life of her, or

perhaps because of it, has no idea what Miller is up to. For her he is a sort of period piece, dragging his overstimulated gonads around the earth, the dusty wake of which attracts a few thousand clods from the "liberated" '60s, climbing aboard his literary phallus and crying "Ship Ahoy" on an ocean of sperm, till Kate Millet comes along in 1969 to set the record straight and restore a modicum of justice to this pariah of women and his coterie of Hugh Hefner clones. "Few would deny the greatness of his Paris books," Dearborn says. But what, exactly, is the nature of this "greatness"? We never find out, but we get hints. Here is one: "The theme of his greatest books is survival, for Miller was first of all a survivor."

That word "survivor," like many of the words she gives the greatest weight to, are buzz words of the '80s, part of the dreary and forbidding lexicon of a stampeded decade. Christ, Mary, Dickie Nixon is a survivor, and he's the best used car salesman we never had. I can walk up any alley in America, the hallway of any institution, and find shells of human beings who have more or less survived. I can start at Columbia University, continue to Congress, and follow a long and sleazy trail to Santa Fe, New Mexico. That's where John Ehrlichman lives. John's doing quite well, thank you. Thanks to advances for books published by our ole buddy, Simon & Schuster. Miller's books aren't about being a survivor at all, Mary. In fact, in one of those books of his that you call a "small success," *The Air Conditioned Nightmare,* Miller addresses that word:

"Few are those who can escape the treadmill. Merely to survive, in spite of the set-up, confers no distinction. Animals and insects survive when higher types are threatened with extinction. To live beyond the pale, to work for the pleasure of working, to grow old gracefully while retaining one's faculties, one's enthusiasm, one's self-respect, one has to establish other values than those endorsed by the mob."

No, no, what we have in Dearborn are precisely those values endorsed by the mob, granted a mob well versed in all the tactics of analysis, articulation, diplomacy, and marketing. The mob I'm talking about splinters into competing groups each week, though all its members have been shaped by the same forces; all clamor for media attention, all speak in shrill, strident voices. Last week it was the Mothers for Abused Little Leaguers, this week it is the Society for Dispossessed White Fire Fighters setting up picket lines in South Albany, Georgia. Tomorrow the Cousins of Cancer Victims will parade in front of Congress. The Jewish Defense League has little interest in baseball or mothers or, for that matter, Lenny Bruce. The so-called feminists (are any of them truly feminine?) don't mention Thoreau or Dick Gregory or Chekhov, who in a letter to a friend said, "There are times when I awake full of euphoria; then I go down to the street and hear a woman's story and grief overwhelms me." Black leaders see no point in the visions of Black Elk, and the smoldering Indians on the Rosebud reservation haven't the faintest idea who Toussaint L'Ouverture is. The environmentalists read tracts, not poetry. But the most indicative remarks about what's really going on in this society come from the mouths of babes. More than one of my students when I taught at Howard University advised me that Richard Wright made a mistake in making the hero of *Native Son,* Bigger Thomas, a dropout. "He should have been a lawyer, then we would have listened," one girl told me, and a number of other students in the class nodded.

. There we have it. It is not vision that counts, but correctness—the code of a society so physically and spiritually mangled you won't meet two people in a given year who know how to walk. The center of gravity in the stride of a U.S.er is in the shoulders. His real hero is the middle linebacker from Notre Dame. For power is what it is all about, not the real power born of experience as it filters to the bone marrow and out again in hard-won articulation, but the specious power of GROUP. Not the GROUP of community, which has a common and noble purpose but the GROUP that wants to aggrandize itself because every member has had his ego pummeled since the day he entered first grade. Not the GROUP that approaches the microphone with a certain caution and with hesitancy as to how it will phrase its grievances, but the GROUP with the pent-up rage of a mob, demanding this and demanding that but asking little of itself as GROUP or as individuals. "More jobs! Education!" is often the battlecry, but Miller, as well as the other visionaries listed here, knew the jobs to be at best a form of masturbation if not downright destructive; education taught us how to vote for one among a series of idiots indistinguishable from one another. In a group of 20 freshmen at Howard, I was lucky to meet one who has ever been encouraged to write or talk about his experiences by one of his previous 50 teachers. What replaces the language of experience and reflection upon that experience is the language of Slogan. The same as TV, newspapers, our daily conversations. Shortcut language in the feverish race to arrive at a goal titled Society's Stamp of Approval. In the meantime, our ears and noses blow out the car window. Never mind, we're in a state of frenzy at a loss we can't remember, but just ahead...just ahead is the exit number for the town of our final arrival. We can't remember the exact number because it gets all confused with the lottery number we played this morning. Life is always happening just outside of us. To start the day, we read the *New York Times* or the *Washington Post* so we are versed in the group-think of separate grievances. We don't begin by wiggling our toes in the grass or staring up and marveling at the sky or carrying *Native Son* to work with us. That would be bad for business. Bigger Thomas, as both a creation of Richard Wright's bloodstream and a piece of independent magic, sees and talks with more power than a thousand Ph.D.s in comparative literature. The entire population of lawyers in Washington, D.C., could fit into his back pocket. Yet if Bigger Thomas wanted to get away with murder today—granted, an accidental one—he wouldn't have to retreat to the rooftops of Chicago. All he would have to do is attach a Walkman to his ears and look numb, walk a puppy on a leash, or pretend he was jogging. The cops wouldn't stop him, nor would any biographer label him a misogynist. You see, Bigger would be offering those evidences that he was thoroughly domesticated, every ounce of the wildness necessary for a vision of happiness and peace gutted out of him by the time he was 12 years old. His struggle to be a man is what we most fear. What Dearborn most fears about Miller. Because she and we are reminded that we make a game of life rather than playing it for real, thus making ourselves shells long before our deaths.

To the young today, Orson Welles is that hustler for a fruity vine, Dick Gregory has a fat farm in the Bahamas, James Earl Jones is the voice on CNN, and Paul Robeson sang gospel songs. Lenny Bruce ran a dirty mouth during a freer time, Emma Goldman inspired commies and did time, Helen Keller invented Braille, Eugene Debs inspired workers during a time when they had no rights, and Henry Thoreau liked to walk in the woods and commune with nature. The casual vacuuming of a casual history of *isms* and sects as it arrives in our living rooms beside the *crepe de carnage,* the Beaujolais, and the stereo offering us a string quartet from heaven. With each passing generation more domesticity sifts down, the passing faces on an average day more seared with rancor and underlying bafflement. We say, "You can't yell fire in a crowded theater," as I will be accused of here. We don't remember that Justice Oliver Wendell Holmes said it upon sentencing Eugene Debs to a year and a day in prison for telling young men not to sign up for the draft in WWI. We don't remember Debs' response either: "Your Honor, 1 was advising young men not to enter a building on fire."

Henry Miller advised us that the whole world was on fire, as well as his heart, the latter unnecessarily so. Like Debbs, he asked us not to get burned. And for this he was and is sentenced with silence and anonymity. When someone like Dearborn steps forth on the privileged support of several powerful institutions to speak of Miller, she rolls us a severely and diligently polished imitation pearl from the persistent vacuum of her own guts and the institutions whose creed she has adopted. From the shallowest depths, this pearl whispers, "It was just a momentary jarring. The man was a mess. Go back to your indentured comfort and everything will be all right."

To whom does the future belong, the three or four Millers who periodically come along, or the legions of Dearborns with their brilliant expertise and inherent cruelty? The answer is neither.

In no field today would we even recognize a leader who could show us the way out of the morass we have gotten ourselves into. Real power abhors a real vacuum, and don't think for a second that the foxy resumes of the Dearborns fill this vacuum. The real power will come in the form of the Crips and Bloods and a dozen other gangs fighting over turf. The difference is that the turf will be the suburbs, the universities, Wall Street, and the airports. Everywhere. These gangs' notion of power is as imitative and reactionary as Dearborn's, the Pentagon's, that of the whole link of institution to institution and the institutional thinking that dominates the U.S. But there's one important difference. They are willing to put their bodies on the line. They have not been funneled through institution after institution so that they can sever word from deed. These are the left-out ones who snicker at the mention of school. What can any teacher teach them, who have organized and plotted and robbed and murdered and lived as if each day were their last. They know in the bat of an eyelash that no adult has anything to offer them, that words from adults are just so much ca-ca running down the side of a building, a building like Simon & Schuster's on the Avenue of the Americas, where they could never enter except through the use of force. And they know the world is run by pure force, not words, not vision, not the poetry of Miller and Thoreau. They don't want any part of the system except to pillage in it in order to create their own system. And their own system will make the SS look like disciples of Billy Graham.

I got a primer on this one the other night on the PBS show *Hate*, chaired by Bill Moyers. During an hour and a half of one expert after another, from John Kenneth Galbraith to Elie Wiesel to the psychiatrist Robert Jay Lifton, experts reflecting on dozens of groups struggling for equality, only three people emerged with any insight into the origin of hatred. The rest circled and circled hate in a dazzling gamut of abstraction.

One of the three was a former Israeli soldier who beat and dragged a Palestinian boy onto a truck in front of his parents. He was later so horrified by the expressions on the faces of those parents that he changed his identity. He reinvented himself in the form of a Palestinian and experienced all the injustice, physical and psychological, that he'd formerly inflicted. "The worst part," he said, "was not the physical abuse but the sense of being a nobody. Even when people were nice to me I had the feeling I didn't exist." What I want to emphasize is that this man experienced the denial of himself not as an Israeli—he'd switched identities—nor as a Palestinian—he could always revert back to at least a semblance of his former existence—but as a man marooned, an individual. Now, on PBS, he speaks as a man living between cultures, a no-man's land, as it were, as a true individual. His body was denied in previous times; if he is to rediscover his body, and the beginnings of freedom, he must approach the world as an individual reaching out for other individuals.

Is this not what Miller was saying? Gregory, Thoreau, Bruce, Goldman, Whitman?

As Miller points out, if anyone comes along to sing "The Body Electric," he is quickly fitted with a skullcap and marched to the electric chair at Sing-Sing prison.

Unless, that is, he sings on behalf of GROUP, a group determined to be as ruthless in its defense and propagation as the next GROUP. Thus enter our final two witnesses, the head of the Crips and the head of the Bloods. Both spoke of hatred as beginning and ending with the body. "Once you deface your enemy in your mind, it's easy to kill him because he didn't really exist before the killing," said the head of the Crips. He added, "It's just like you sending boys to Vietnam and telling them to kill gooks. They're gooks, they don't have faces. Well, it's the same for us with our enemies."

There is no doubt that the Crips and the Bloods and a

hundred other gangs mean to turn this hatred inside them on the world; they are already doing it. There are no men and women around worth the name to stop them, and had there been, there would not have been cause for the Crips and the Bloods to have been born in the first place. For two centuries now we've been resisting every fresh voice that came down the road, labeling them this and labeling them that, even as a former civilization created layer after layer of slave society and for all its sophistication received as its reward Huns and Visigoths. Do we deserve better?

kiss me, i'm still alive:
on irving stettner

If you want to wake up happy in the morning, read Irving Stettner. If your nerve endings are frayed, your mouth dry, and you're alone because your mate just flew the coop with your best friend's mother, read Stettner. Stettner will flush your liver, tap on your nasal passages, and make your hormones burgeon like overripe plums. You will wake in the morning feeling a lightness, openness, and generosity you haven't known in years. But such attributes here in dear old Weenyville can only make you subject to arrest. No longer rigid with YIP's syndropme (Yuppies In search of Power), you can only take up residence in a jail cell, but make certain to take a copy of Stettner with you.

For Stettner is the original street urchin. And has remained one for 70 years. He is a man without a Social Security card because he has little interest in security and he has never bought the noxious socializing process that informs most of our souls. He lives out of two suitcases in one-room apartments where the gas jets on the two-burner stove are clogged from the overflow of pea soup.

He has no car, no insurance policies, no Walkman, and only the faintest notion of how he will earn his rent due the following week. A helluva way to live, you say? No, the joke is on us, for Stettner's life testifies to the power and joy we could achieve if we lost our fear of poverty. In the words of William James, "Our stocks might fall, our hopes of promotion vanish, our salaries stop, our club doors close in our faces; yet, while we lived, we would imperturbably bear witness to the spirit, and our example would help to set free our generation."

That is precisely what Stettner's work bears testament to—"witness to the spirit"—or, more precisely, a spirit that keeps his head raised and his eyes and ears delighting in much of what he sees and hears. The term "memoirs" isn't quite appropriate to his non-poetry works. They are little philosophies of action that form a consistent whole. Their genesis is not literally inspired, but comes from a desire to be alive. We are born to take part in life, not to drain meaning from it, not to arrange it in preconceived forms. Moment-by-moment impulse and a constant alertness to everything that has fullness and movement are the heart of Stettner's writing. He has retained the joy and wonder of childhood in a country that specializes in turning out perpetual adolescents who have lost every virtue of childhood. In short, Stettner is an innocent traveling among a nation of parasites. He creates; we consume, convinced by all sorts of idiots posing as experts that the "creative spirit" belongs to a select few who are first sent to "gifted classes," later take advanced placement English, and eventually win a National Book Award, a Booker Prize, or a Nobel. This is the approved version of "creativity" and acquaints us with all the mannerisms of art but none of its power. "In real art," says Picasso, "painting isn't an aesthetic operation; it's a form of magic designed as a mediator between this strange, hostile world and us, a way of seizing power by giving form to our terrors as well as our desires."

Today, readers and writers are trained alike; language is a form of deflection, not a way of "seizing power." To be a real reader or a real writer, one would have to both burn off the institutionalized forms of dead grass, as the

Indians used to do, and re-create new ways of approaching the written word.

Because our lives have become so abstract, so removed from both earth and heaven, we offer each other opinions and arguments, not stories.

As a parallel to the breakdown in literature, and by way of showing the strange route Stettner has taken toward discovering both life and the written word, let's take copulating. People complain to me all the time about the treatment they get at the hands of the opposite sex. Women complain about the deviousness of men. Men complain about the deviousness of women. Both sexes complain about their inability to find good fucking. In a world where the inflation of language makes all subjects spurious, it's the one topic people agree is worth talking about.

Yet, never do I hear from people that the approaches to fucking are all screwed up. By approaches, I mean the places and avenues through which we meet our potential copulating partners, namely the workplace, bars, and parties. Each of those little meeting places fosters a language which is doomed to efficiency, and the cunt and the cock and true art abhor a language which is efficient. The language of efficiency ignores the passions and thwarts the pituitary. It is a language that fosters not creativity but equivocating: "Maybe yes, and maybe no, and everywhere all over. Where did you say you worked?" Equivocating is the language of business. The language of business has only one desire: to find a sucker. As President Coolidge once said, "The chief business of the American people is business," and it was a statement more prophetic than any poet uttered in the 20th century.

The bars, the parties, and the workplace don't establish warmth or intimacy. They are as cold as any meat locker. No wonder then, in a place like Weenyville (Washington, D.C.), it is possible to meet thousands of handsome people, well-educated, finely tuned to the arts, the men speaking in the crisp modulations of a Gregory Peck, the women as poised as the queens of the soap operas, and not discover a drop of juice in any one of them. To hear them talk after seven beers, you'd get the impression they could take on a chorus line or the Green Bay Packers in a single night, but all the physical evidence suggests they would be better off at home with their computers.

Now you see why all that is called serious literature is up Shit Creek. The approaches to writing, as with the approaches to copulating, are totally wrong. Born in the schools, students of writing travel a vertical route through layer after layer of equivocating, which is to say the business of art is business; you can be as funny and truthful as you want, but if you don't make a good buck, or at least win a few awards with your stories, you can go fuck yourself. We'll all stay at home and hump our Apples till we learn the art of proper equivocating. A Washington, D.C. restauranteur named Benny once advised me, "Where you have money, there's no action." The man spoke wisdom.

Year after year, Jonathan Yardley of the *Washington Post* bemoans the breakdown in contemporary American fiction, but you won't catch Jonathan reviewing Stettner's work. Yardley's assertions to the contrary, he rarely reviews small press work. He doesn't search out good books to review; he reviews what comes to him. And what comes to him are the same frozen meat lockers for literature that are offered to us to find our potential fucking partners: hardback books from the big conglomerates in New York and Boston, accompanied by publicists' handouts.

This, in turn, is backed by nationwide distribution, the cooperation of the bookstore chains, the economic clout of the wholesalers, the tepid and sniveling readings and workshops at the universities, and finally the you-pat-my-bum-and-I'll-pat-yours kind of reviewing that goes on in the major newspapers and magazines. Periodically a Yardley is held up as a legitimate critic and offered in defense of the criticism that a place like the *Post* is going soft. Yet, Yardley is no different than the Gregory Peck modulators at parties who, after seven beers, quack "There is no good fucking in this town." Presented with a good book or a good woman, they couldn't recognize it as such, and if they did, they couldn't get a hard on anyway. The gulf between word and action has been legitimized. Indeed, the whole system by which we drowse in our comforts and pick our noses depends on it.

For the exact meeting point where the institution of reviewing and all the other institutions meet, I'll let Kurt Vonnegut talk for awhile. In an April 29, 1990, letter to me, Vonnegut discusses a particular review he wrote for the *New York Times* and, by implication, how that institution functions: "I wrote a review of Tom Wicker's book about Attica [the prison riot in which scores of inmates were slaughtered], and they knocked off the last third of it without first telling me. The last third was about why Wicker cried when the shooting started." The *New York Times* doesn't want tears from a grown man. It's afraid of tears, terrified out of its living skull of tears. Nor does it want real joy, real despair, real anything. Where all the institutions meet is their utter fear and dismay at emotion. Animal or human, sooner or later they find a way to shoot emotion.

Thus, there is a superb irony here. Though the artist begins from emotional impulses, the institutions designed to support art have a chronic and perverse fear of emotion. If more than a hint of the raw emotional life that goes into a painting or a novel (or the messiness at somehow surviving while you get your creative work accomplished) is displayed, the supposed benefactors of art and artists run from the room, mumbling, "Taste, what's become of taste?" The adventurous artist will not find support among art institutions, and rarely among his supposed fellow artists. No, he will find it where he least expects it: the food and beverage manager at a dreary and pompous hotel chain, a computer expert, a hairdresser, the checkout girl at the supermarket, the bakery women—black and poor and overworked—at the same supermarket. Such people have not bought the official line on art. Though they have limited means of supporting art, they know it must originate in the heart. They often write poems or paint pictures which remain hidden from even their families and mates. This is not a world which looks on the amateur with much respect or sympathy.

To be called a real artist, a "professional," you have to get your work out in front of people and get paid for it. To earn this prestigious title, both the artist and his work must first be screened through an elaborate daisy chain of de-genitalized idiots with the right connections, all of whom believe art is a civilizing maneuver. It has become respectable to be an artist, and the artist in turn must be respectable. The number of people who want to be writers or painters is legion, each of them so brain-dead, they are ready at a whisper to pare their overwrought emotions to manageable proportions if only it will ensure, if not success, a little respectability. Respectability is when you get in on a group show or when you place a poem in the magazine Swollen Tendril. Never mind what the gallery or magazine, newspaper, arts council, or university ultimately stands for. "Get me some attention and legitimize me, or I'll piss all over my neighbor's petunias," the fledgling artist says to himself.

The extent to which the artist must be respectable offers no better example than our long-neglected subject under the microscope here, Irving (Oivin to his friends) Stettner. Early in September, I got a call from a faculty member at UCLA we will call Bill Williams. This is the centennial of Henry Miller's birth, and in the last week of this month writers and professors and others will be celebrating him with seminars and conferences up and down the West Coast. Williams said he was part of a panel that was going to discuss the legacy of Miller. He had read my essay on Miller, and wanted to know if I would be willing to serve on the panel. This discussion stalled when it became uncertain whether UCLA would be willing to put up travel expenses. At some point in the conversation, I asked Snyder why he didn't invite Irving Stettner to this conference on the legacy of Henry Miller. His response: "Stettner's a bit scruffy, isn't he?"

Never mind that Stettner had exchanged more than a hundred letters with Miller; never mind that Stettner was one of the few people that Miller thought of as a real friend; never mind that Stettner's tiny literary magazine *Stroker* was one of the few in which Miller would publish his work the last three years of his life. And never mind that Stettner has written and painted brilliantly all his life, that he has had to find his audience by going from cafe to cafe, bar to bar in New York's Lower East Side, including Alphabet City—one of the most drug-ridden and dangerous places in America—hawking his paintings and books. A dollar here, a dollar there, anything to stave off the landlord for another week. Stettner, with his bulbous work shoes and broken umbrella, plods along in the rain, looking for someone to put a touch on, while Williams, in casually mussed tweeds, smokes his pipe, chirps to a classroom full of students about the "mavericks of art," and casually blows smoke out his ass.

Ten days after our phone conversation, a packet arrived from Williams. In it was a videocassette entitled *The Henry Miller Odyssey*, a film portrait of a "diabolically truthful man" by . . . Bill Williams. Much of the film centers on Miller's Paris days, when he begged, borrowed, and stole to survive and produce those books that some people call "art," days when it could be surely said of Miller that he was "scruffy." Miller from his grave and Stettner from his easel are chuckling at such whorehouse shenanigans as celebrations and seminars. They know that as soon as a writer gets invited to such things, he is dead. Surely the brochure produced for the celebration illustrates Celine's statement, "Every virtue has its own indecent literature."

Even more deadly is the language of equivocating that reduces everyone to the same level. Fear reduces language to a steady, dreary sludge of ambiguity, is what the American Melting Pot is all about. Everything and everyone is flattened under the ethic of efficient modernity, which finally adds up to downright worship of The Machine. Listen to the low rumble of slick, cunning, evasive language coming from the mouths of everyone concerned in those televised Senate hearings on the confirmation of Clarence Thomas. (In 1991 Thomas was a conservative Black who was eventually confirmed to the Supreme Court despite controversy over supposed sexual harassment of an employee ten years earlier.) Listen to these hearings and you realize this is the language of fife and fickle, foam and dome, and till death do us part you'll never know what I'm thinking. It's not merely the flattening of human fiber and bone, but the steady, cautious erasure of every vestige of human personality. It is the language of the professional workplace, not in the service of expansiveness of blood vessel, but padded non-talk to win a grant, protect a position, create an image. In such a hopelessly gray world as the workplace, there is nothing else to do but periodically cry, "Long Dong Silver." In such a world, everyone is harassed because every human being is interchangeable with every other human. No one counts, only the system, a system that has no use for the direct language, the rage and delight of Whitman or Thoreau or Stettner, only for the bubble-gum language of law books written by men with hippo jowls, laws entitling them to stuff more poison down their gullets.

The whole point in getting powerful jobs is power, to be boss, to make others obey their will, leverage in the service of ego, and, yes, sex. "Up on Capitol Hill, they used to fuck right on the desk tops," offers a lawyer after several drinks one night, who said he had 15 years experience on the Hill. "Now, with all the flak from discrimination and sexual harassment suits, they take them to a hotel room."

In 1991, most Americans are afraid of strangers; the one place where they overcome their fear of other people is the workplace. Work is where most people make their social base. This explains why marriage, initially born of at least some small intimacy, quickly degenerates into a business partnership. The language of equivocation wins out entirely; each partner pretends the other doesn't have genitals, let alone a sense of humor. Then, divorce, and the whole process begins again. But, this time around, the beleaguered divorcee swears he is not going to invest so much of his heart. He'll invest his energies in a career where the heart is not as much at risk. Career is the language of law books, business manuals, and academic jargon. If the pulsations of groin beckon, our career soul has only to interrupt them before they get to the heart, before they involve the whole person; he has only to bark at some underling, "Wanna see a picture of a chicken going down on a stripper?" Of course, dear underling could always say, "It's chickens who should be eaten, and preferably fried. Now cut the shit and hand me that file folder." But underling doesn't. She answers in the professional jargon of ambiguity; her whole training has been not to offend the boss; besides, only through such language can she advance her "professional" career. She says, "At this point in time, I believe categorically that the civil rights of both the chicken and the stripper are in jeopardy." Boss is sitting there thinking, "Is this bitch for real?" though this is exactly how he would phrase the issue if he were not in rutting season. "Maybe she is putting me on, maybe she's in heat too and this is just code talk for 'I'm available'; I'll ask her out and maybe then I'll have some idea where she's coming from." And on and on.

Nobody in that Senate committee room (Clarence Thomas confirmation hearings) had the faintest idea what anybody was saying. Constantly they asked each other to repeat a question or an answer; explanation was offered to explain explanation, and with each succeeding drone and dribble of cautious rhetoric, they dug a deeper and deeper hole. Of course the senators can't make a decision; neither can we. The wrong people are on trial. The people who should be made to defend themselves are Thomas's and Hill's law and writing professors at Yale. They would each be given three minutes to tell a story—not an argument—that everyone could understand. If they failed to do so, Ted Kennedy could step down from the rostrum and yank out their tongues with a pair of pliers.

Watch the faces of the senators, particularly Kennedy. They are bored to tears. For 40 years they have been listening to such horse-shit. They are bored with their jobs, bored with so many words, bored with all the toxins their livers are spewing up from too much rich food and booze. When Anita Hill said, "I was both disgusted and embarrassed," it didn't register. Only when she got to the part about pictures of animals and Thomas' alleged references to his prodigious dong ("Long Dong Silver") did they perk up. All the rest was a charade for our benefit, to get our vote, and more importantly to convince us that it was business as usual. The real obscenity was that most people have been conned out of their very lives; these same people sat and watched these assholes for hours at a time, fully trusting that the legislation they draft next week or next year is going to protect them in some way. Along with Kennedy, the senators and a good portion of the viewing audience were all so sunk in tedium that inwardly they were smiling and wondering to themselves, "Just how big is this guy's dick?" Where quality of life evaporates, quantity rears its sniveling head. It's called objectivity. "We are gathering all the evidence we can so we can arrive at an objective decision," one senator cried from the podium. Yes, you can be objective, senator; you can go home and pound your pudding in a bucket of Mother's Oats.

But if you, the reader, want to know what is really going on in this capital of capitals, listen to this 25-year old graduate of the University of Chicago, recently arrived in Washington, D.C., to work in one of the many "think tanks" that abound here: "Washington has a way of attracting the most intelligent young people and then co-opting their intelligence into the existing system. Each day I go to work, I realize it's all a lot of bullshit. My job revolves around my boss. The other day, he handed me a pass to a meeting at the White House; the week before it was two tickets to the Kennedy Center. I get paid well, and there are always these perks. The whole point is to follow on the boss's coattails because he has the connections to keep your career moving. I know it is all wrong, but I don't have an alternative vision."

It may be that this young man does not have an alternative vision because he hasn't gotten miserable enough to desire to look for one. He is a devoted reader of offbeat fiction but apparently none of the books suggest to him that he might live differently. Probably these books are called "Literature": they are clever and they amuse him but they are, after all, just books. What he needs is a tonic that would give him another vision of life and develop in him the patience to develop a language to support that vision. He needs writers and painters like Stettner.

But as I've shown here, Stettner does not count. He is "scruffy." He is outside the system. If you want to advance in a career, image is what counts. Along the way, you had better find the specious, insulated, non-language to support that career.

If our young friend wants an alternative vision to dependency on the Boss and the Boss's accompanying conveyor belt of smugness, comfort, and utterly joyless existence, he might glance at the work of Stettner. Stettner is the antithesis of everything the young man has been taught. He is the opposite of the wall to knowing yourself or to the world as I have described it.

Stettner is more a descendant of Mozart and Chagall than any writer. He is eighty feet off the ground, and at night he floats over the rooftops of Paris, Manhattan, Tokyo, and LA. The sky is blue-black; there is a full moon; and there is Stettner, playing violin on the rooftop of his favorite whorehouse. In Colon, Panama, he falls in love with a prostitute, and stays in love with her even after she gives him two doses of the clap. Is Stettner a fool? Of course! But no more a fool than a Chaplin, Keaton, or W.C. Fields. He is the eternal innocent who takes life where he can find it and always makes a song of it. "He looks on the gorgeous side of shit without ever denying that all of us have a very difficult life to live these days" says Seymour Krim (also a remarkable writer) about Stettner.

It is not that he has blundered into that soap bubble that says, "Let's look on the positive side of life," but that he is insistent on being faithful to an endless curiosity and exuberance and, above all, to maintaining a freedom of movement unshackled by the bread cupboard or by ideological enterprises. He is that rarest of creatures, a free man. By free, I mean he has faith—not faith in the religious cliche of that word, but faith that he can find both in men and in nature the expansiveness that will make him feel glad to be alive. And Stettner finds it everywhere.

But mainly he finds it in the street. If Stettner has a religion, it is The Street, accompanied by the son and the holy ghost of The Incident and The Stranger.

Anywhere in the world now, the entire machinery of education, govermnent, and media is devoted to one thing: convincing people that the streets are dangerous and that they should stay home and, by inference, turn over their lives to some polite, sophisticated, crackpot institution (i.e. themselves). Occasionally, in some rap song, I get a notion that there is something to be learned in the streets besides bloodshed, but no other medium advances such subversive knowledge. Take away the streets and you take away freedom of movement, people's innocence, their right to gaze, create, respond, discover anything new. If the 19th century is the study of how the people, often in a misguided form, took the streets from the king and queen, the 20th century is the study of how they returned the streets to a series of "democratic" institutions that supposedly represented the interests of the people, but found increasingly ingenious ways to get people off the street. They have succeeded, because most towns and cities in the U.S. at 6:30 on any given evening are deserts of concrete and glass. Cross the border from Mexico into the United States, and cleanliness and order strike the eye, not life. The great science of the 20th century, then, is not nuclear fission or aerodynamics but crowd control refined to the point of crowd elimination.

Control the streets and you control how people eat, shit, fuck, and count their money; you control how people think and feel. In a stadium or concert hall, there are walls; the crowd is contained; the same with a university, office complex, or shopping mall. Only the street offers a free flow where there is easy means of entrance and escape. Like the arteries of the body, the street can literally sing with fresh infusions of blood, or it can get wounded, become infected, and bit by bit have its various limbs develop gangrene. It doesn't just die, the dead part is chopped off and thrown on the scrap heap. Thus, in addition to crowd control, which is the duty of every true professional, the next most proliferating science of the 20th century is surgery. This surgeon comes in the form of doctors, cops, hangmen, prison wardens, and teachers. All their training teaches them to be objective. Only the funeral parlor director is objective. Surgery and crowd control become one and the same thing.

Most of the supposed revolutionaries, including Marx, who want to dynamite the blockaded ends of the streets to allow a true flow of blood, have been another in the series of surgeons and crowd control ignoramuses. They don't want a free flow of blood; they want type A blood or type B blood, never circulation. The rubble from the explosion of this or that political fixation creates new blockages under this or that fashionable label, and the whole dreary process starts again.

"Europe, it seems to us, is also close to saturation and aspires, tired as she is, to settle, to crystallise out, finding her stable social position in a *petty, mean mode of life*." [italics in the original]. This statement was made in 1852 by a wandering Russian named Alexander Herzen. Does it not describe the United States today? The "settled" or "stable social position" can be observed in any bar where the patrons stare up at the television like catatonic zombies to gauge the progress of the latest competitive feast; or in any classroom where students sit with their notebooks folded, their hands folded, their brains folded, waiting to "be turned on" by some card-carrying Ph.D who folded up 20 years ago; or in any office where the recipients of patronage wait for the boss to give the word on which color toilet paper they should wipe with this week.

It is all the same. We are all the same. Waiting like Godot for some one or some thing to turn us on. Make us feel alive, like we're breathing, and blood does really flow in our veins. We sit, waiting for the cry of "Long Dong Silver" to break us up, make us laugh and applaud with relief, because in that small portion of our hearts still receiving blood we know the public obscenity and the private will are one and the same, reducible to a stale joke. Any other cry, any other language with a hint of intelligence and imagination couldn't penetrate our brains, loggered as they are with bad air, bad beer, bad pizza, insufferable slogans, and not the faintest notion of what it is to be a human being.

"The life of a student is more full of incidents and proceeds much more stormily than the sober, workman-like life of the father of a family," Herzen continues. "A life without incidents, sometimes diverted by external impulses, would be reduced to a uniform rotation, to a faintly varying *semper idem*. Parliament would assemble, the budget would be presented, forms improved...and the next year it would be the same, and the same ten years later."

Stettner does not have the problems of sameness because he is a seeker and a giver who employs his trade on the street. He is a sidewalk sketch artist, and as such, his life is filled not with just strangers, but with an alertness to the amazing variety of human beings. Without such an awareness, an affection for the bonding of the eccentric and the bond broker (as Balzac often saw), we go mad. We become numb and intolerant if we cannot find and love the peculiarities of eccentrics as they nibble the sharp edges of Dollar and the assumptions of people who have Dollar.

Often, before he made his rounds of the Paris cafes to sketch people, Stettner warmed up with trees, flowers, and plants in a nearby park. Then, when he sketched people, he saw them in another way: "If I ran into the most nondescript, ugliest mug imaginable: I was always able to find one feature, at least—I simply looked for it—which had a spark of beauty to it." This is not arresting beauty for the sake of money or simply a Pollyanna outlook to spare himself reality; Stettner understands that the source of energy, hence his own salvation, is located precisely at some detail of grace. Let the grace of a chin or pair of eyes blossom and the whole person has a reborn look. Thus, Stettner's flatteries become suggestions for revival. The only problem was tbat people took on a slightly hollyhock look after he had been to the park. When he looked at people he saw flowers, and his clients stared at the finished portraits "perplexedly a few minutes, until they finally shrug their shoulders, and smile indifferently, as if chalking it off to my uniquely individual style."

What excitement Stettner feels when he has a good day—is able to feed himself, have a glass of wine, knows he can stay in his hotel room another two days. And what an embarrassment to us who make nothing, who shuffle papers with a dead language to validate other papers equally dead, and return to our apartments assured of eating. Stettner grows while we languish, feasting on public issues we think will lend our lives importance.

The best part of The Street is that incident leads to incident, stranger to stranger. He meets a bookseller, who in turn leads him to a Greek artist named Kosta. Kosta rips the young Stettner's assumptions about life while paying him money to sketch the streets of Paris: "Artist—gad, you don't even know the meaning of the word...Also, you're an American; that's nine strikes against you. You think you can do everything by pressing a button...no patience! ...And *you* meanwhile. It's getting so cold, you said, a little while ago, 'tomorrow you're going to wear two sweaters.' Imagine! My, my....Why, do you know the kind of men in whose footsteps you're following? Giotto, Van Gogh, Gauguin...Guys who tore their guts out, and slapped them on to canvas!"

At age 18 or 25, we should all be so lucky to have such a virulent and invigorating criticism to wean us from our whining. Hah! Try such uncompromising language on a group of young people today and they will telephone their lawyer fathers to press for a "harassment" lawsuit.

What evolves in Stettner is a devotion to moment-by-moment living—the air, the sky, food, the flow of a particular woman, wine—and the variety and quality such things yield. He is not looking over his shoulder to see if a grant, a gallery showing, an editor waving a contract are pursuing him. He goes to Tokyo and the small towns of Japan: "The Japanese women. Yes, just to small towns of Japan: "The Japanese women. Yes, just to be able to sit opposite one in a trolley car was an experience in itself, unforgettable. There was the full round rich moon oval of their faces, each with its delicate finely chiseled nose and mouth, and the slanted jewel eyes."

He goes to Colon, Panama: "I remember Avenida Bolivar, its long, wide-open main street with its unique heavy sweet smell of chicory, dust, dung, mangos, and palm fronds all intermixed, the swinging louvered doors of the porticoed bamboo shops and bars, the hot sun beating down like a laughing gold tom-tom, the high shoeshine parlor chairs right out in the street, the shoeshine boys' lively chatter in broken English and Spanish."

Stettner is sort of like horseshit: he turns up everywhere, except that unlike manure, his eyes and ears and heart get bigger and bigger, the writing a little more patient with each volume, without sacrificing the exuberance or sharp details that capture the essence of place—family while growing up in Brooklyn; the utter vacuum of the streets of Los Angeles as he knocks on doors, a kind of Fuller Brush salesman. He wears the pavements on his sleeve, and he is pure tonic because he is conscious of the vitality, even when it's deranged, within the bullies as well as the more kindly souls of this earth.

These portraits of people and places are written the way Stettner makes pictures: quick, bold lines built around two or three central features and colored with his enthusiasm for the subject. Like Henry Miller, Stettner gives me the feeling of a companion chatting away. But while Miller is content to rap away in some cafe corner, Stettner is perpetually looking for space. The movement is from the streets and doings of men and women to the tops of buildings, trees, sky with its own incessant change. In particular he loves the sea; it is natural that he spent several years as a seaman. The world of the sea and sky is much more tolerant of rhapsodizing—of growing wings and taking deep breaths—than office buildings or subways.

The stories in these books are not just about survival—the hand-to-mouth existence of hundreds of odd jobs and survival's relief through a painterly vision of the heavens, but about the men and women in his life who have helped shape a voluptuous attitude toward daily activity. A couple of the men are famous, like Miller and Stieglitz, but mostly they are unknown—construction helpers, seamen, unknown artists, whorehouse madams and their charges, a zany uncle, two teachers, and a music shop owner. They are distinguished and held together by a Mediterranean attitude toward life. By their robust affection for food, wine, the human body, and protest in action against injustice—not just in words—they keep Stettner earthbound and from settling on a cloud with his Aeolian harp. On the subjects of manhood and art, they freely dispense advice to the young Stettner. Just as valuable, they are always buying the little fucker something to eat. Between Miller and Stettner, 1 swear the prerequisite for adventure and art is an empty stomach and an equally empty wallet. Everywhere Stettner goes, he gets himself adopted.

Alfred Stieglitz is famous now as a photographer and as the husband of Georgia O'Keeffe, but 50 years ago his gallery on Manhattan, An American Place, was lucky to get two visitors a day. One of those was young Irving. When Stettner complains to Stieglitz that he has no money to buy a Marin painting, the owner says to him, "Never mind, someday you'll pay the price."

49

"What do you mean?"

"Everyone pays—sooner or later. One can't receive without giving in return—in one form or another. Especially you—since you're born with a gift, and quite a precious one, too, like a jewel, which sooner or later you'll have to give. Or share, rather, since that's what gifts are for. It's simply your fate: you'll be miserable till you do."

Stettner doesn't understand what Stieglitz is talking about. His memoirs, then, can be viewed as the attempt to fulfill his advisor's prophecy, to understand the nature of what he has to offer and the price he must pay for answering his destiny. Nowhere is he more miserable than when he can't summon the courage to marry a beautiful Japanese girl named Emiko, with whom he has fallen in love. He loses not just the girl through his own cowardice but a whole way of life he loves just as passionately as the girl.

As Emiko presents herself the first time, she is pure grace and sureness, an antidote to Stettner's descriptions of American life, which is often pure bullying and arrogance born out of confusion:

"She dropped to her knees, and, head erect, with slow and graceful gestures served us tea. Bright auras of jeweled silence seemed to float around her...I was entranced, speechless: she was like a flower, a tiger lily or chrysanthemum, swaying at the end of its long stem...one of those women who don't have to speak since their faces say everything: enigmatic, exquisitely beautiful, totally feminine, yet feline, demonically so...."

She releases in Stettner his first desire to draw in three years; he draws his love and presents it to Emiko's family. "I watched them as they eyed it with broad, appreciative smiles. What a difference, I reflected, between their reaction to my pencil sketch, and that of my own parents back in Brooklyn...My mother and father would have regarded it with total indifference. Either that, or they would deeply wrinkle their foreheads and roll their eyeballs heavenward, as if uttering a silent prayer, as if I had only presented them with a grim omen of my fate: in life I was headed straight for the penniless gutter."

All this takes place a few months after the U.S. dropped atomic bombs on Hiroshima and Nagasaki. Emiko's parents would have had every right to close the door to an American soldier trying to woo their daughter. Instead, they treat Stettner with courtesy and hospitality, and it's not because he brings chocolate and cigarettes (mediums of exchange in postwar Japan) to their home. It's because he is sincere, handles himself with tact, and offers curiosity and respect toward their way of life. On his last evening with them, he thinks, "ahead lies a shaky wooded house which shelters a few friends with whom I've known the first real happiness and contentment of my life."

Yet, Stettner is easily convinced to turn his back on his love and her family. It was necessary in those days to get the permission of the U.S. Army if a soldier wanted to marry.

"Who's the gal?" a captain queries him.

"Emiko Yamada."

"You don't mean a Japanese girl, do you?"

A friend of Stettner's, a private like him, is just as bad.

"Just think," he says, "How are your folks going to feel—if you bring home a Japanese girl?"

Of course, now, 45 years later, the Japanese have had the last word. If they reneged on buying up our Treasury bills, issued quarterly, the entire U.S. economy might fall on its face in a matter of weeks.

Not only has young Stettner still not understood

Stieglitz, but these magical sketches of post-war Japan serve as a cautionary tale. They undercut any facile romanticizing of Stettner's life. Few people realize at the time who or what is of real value. It is only when we build space and reflection into our lives that we understand who can best serve us and what we have to give to gain new value. This takes money and a simpler mode of life, because it takes at least some money to buy the *time* to evaluate what is best for our lives. Someone like Stettner, living on the fly, not sure where his next shelter is coming from, dashing from city to city, country to country, uncertain of his values, loses track of who and what is worth keeping. I believe in many instances it is only in the writing that he rediscovers those gems that have slipped from his fingers. It is a hugely sad story, this tale of the lost Emiko and the patience and tolerance she might have brought to a frantic man's frantic life. But it is no less the story of the United States, a country looked to now for 150 years as the salvation of starved and drained people all over the world, but a country, for all the chit-chat about its melting pot ambience, which has little interest in alternative ways of living.

This is the nagging thread Stettner picks up on in his memoirs. From 1946 to 1968, he runs around the U.S. and half the world snatching for this alternative vision that Emiko first alerted him to in heart and flesh and not just the dictums of Stieglitz. He goes from one job to another, trying to filch a little time to paint and write. His reflections go back to his childhood and the handful of characters and oases within the factory desert of Brooklyn. Most prominent among these are his mother's remarks about a local bum-drunk, whom the child Stettner judges to be disgusting in his louse-ridden clothes and incessant babbling. When he complains to his mother, she says, "You should feel lucky being able to sit

with him. He used to be a musician, and a great one, too."
It's little incidents like this that set off reverberations
throughout Stettner's memoirs. Increasingly he drifts
toward the company of oddballs—the drunks, the mad,
the eccentric, the floaters. In 1968, Stettner claims his
passport was conned from him by a U.S. Embassy
official promising a free trip from Paris to New York.
The U.S. govermnent refused to return it for 15 years,
thus grounding Stettner on the Lower East Side. There he
survived through a hundred odd jobs, wrote and painted
out of a one-room apartment, and hustled his wares
among the bars and cafes of that area. It was there that
he began a lively and profuse correspondence with Henry
Miller and started a literary magazine called *Stroker*.
"Miller must have found here [Lower East Side] a strong
degree of comfort," he says, noting the "verve,
humanness, and European mellowness" on Second
Avenue.

Nearing 70 and still in good health, Stettner has
recently moved to Shaverstown, Pennsylvania. He says
he is working on more Paris memoirs. But I feel it is the
years 1968 to 1991 he should deal with. I say this
because there is a difference between the innocence of
one's youth and "earned innocence," a term invented by
Nelson Algren. It is comparatively easy to be light and
carefree at 24 or 34. During these years, Stettner is a
promising artist. But the United States specializes in and
cultivates youthful potential that never comes to fruition.
Look at all the one-book authors—Styron, Mailer,
Heller, Salinger (one and a half), etc., etc. But how does
anyone keep their gusto, verve, humanness when the gray
hairs settle in and he has an artistic audience of 14, eats
out of tin cans, and buys coarse toilet paper instead of
White Cloud? This is what I mean by earned innocence.

In short, how is it that the boy becomes a man, shakes

off the mentors and becomes a true voice in his own right? To some extent, in his poems Stettner indicates he has retained wide open eyes and a clear, singing voice, but I still feel the fuller treatment that only prose offers is needed to fill out his self-made suit.

I could go on and on about the magic of Stettner, his joy, and his refusal to whine though his material circumstances have been difficult. But the fact is Irving Stettner could not sell his paintings and books on the streets of Washington, D.C., or any other city in America.

He would have to have a vendor's license. Cost—$1,106. That's right, $1,106: $1,000 as a refundable cash bond held by the city should he poison us with a vision of a different kind of life and $106 for a license to sell on our cherished streets. True, he might camp under the protection of some friendly bar or restaurant owner or bookstore manager, but it is the more sympathetic and adventurous business that collapses first. We don't want life; we want power, and we want it fast. The streets have been turned over to two extremes: the real estate speculators and the banks, who have the full support of the corrupt politicians who control the zoning boards; and the teenage street gangs and the drug desperadoes, who are going to cut our throats if we don't hand over our purses or wallets, fast. Though Stettner lived on the Lower East Side of Manhattan for 30 years and was considered a legend there, he can no longer live there. It is too dangerous. "Hell, let him sell his books at Lincoln Center," you say?

Four years ago I witnessed what happens when a writer tries to sell his books at Lincoln Center. Now, New York's vending laws exempt writers and painters, but the police don't know it. On the day I stood beside a newly arrived writer from Toronto selling his self-published novel, four cops hopped out of a cruiser and asked him if he were selling religious books. "Only religious books can be sold on the streets," they told him.

"My book has a spiritual quality," he told them.

"Don't start that intellectual shit with us; get out of here."

He started to gather up his books and display stand, but not fast enough for these contemporary enforcers of what is correct marketing on the streets. One cop pushed him and, when the writer protested verbally, gave him another shove and tripped him. Then the other cops joined the first cop in giving this "unprofessional" writer a few kicks to the ribs. When I jumped between them, I was handcuffed, thrown in the police car, and eventually booked, along with the writer, for disorderly conduct.

The charges were finally dropped, but before we left the station, the cops said, "Keep your asses off the street and this kind of thing won't happen."

Why didn't he or I protest this to the proper authorities?

Why didn't Anita Hill (assuming for a second she is telling the truth) protest "sexual harassment" at the hands of her boss?

"I don't understand," says one senator, "why in this city of all cities, Washington, D.C., where there are so many avenues for redressing grievances, why Anita Hill couldn't have come forward 10 years ago with her story." Because, senator, from the age of two, we are all taught we are little people. Until we are two, senator, we are taught to walk and talk. After the age of two, and for the rest of our lives, we are taught to shut up and sit down. The airing of our "embarrassment and anger" over an injustice at the hands of a superior conflicts with this dictum. From the age of two all we are taught is competition. Winners count, not losers. Power, not language, not true vitality, is what counts. It is not the police or the drug gangs who are to blame. They are the reactionary tools of "professionals" like Williams, who finds Stettner too "scruffy" to include in the party. They are the tools of the well-housed everywhere who use language like "at this point in time," a phrase first popularized by John Dean 16 years ago during other nationally televised hearings. Murder space and time through the "fashionable" use of language and you close off the streets. Now we are just a phrase away from viewing all people as alike under the banner of correct political and racial and sexual thinking. We are ready to assign our emotions to the banner of our "professional careers" and their accompanying language of equivocation and "objectivity."

Now, now, Henry Miller's statement that "Only murderers have profited in the 20th century" makes absolute sense. Close off the streets to people like Stettner, and the cops and the kids are licensed to maim and murder.

Mayor Sharon Pratt Dixon could win "the drug war" in one week. All she would have to do is turn loose 70,000 10-year-olds on the streets of D.C. Let them sing their songs, paint the sides of buildings, dance in front of the restaurants, shout their poems, and run up and down Dupont Circle, playing the flute and the oboe. And let the police escort them in the rougher sections of town. Put the circulating blood of creativity back into the streets and watch the natural "high" that everyone gets. But such an idea will be written off as pie-in-the-sky romanticism, a crackpot notion from a crackpot artist.

Besides, anything involving "art" is consigned to the "appropriate department," but it's the departmentalization of everything that leads to the strangulation of the creative will. Sharon Pratt Dixon, no more than any other supposed leader, has no more idea of what keeps the blood flowing in a city than she does in her own body. She, like the rest of us, has been trained to hate the body. It is a tool, something loathsome that must be hammered into submission to sit at a desk, a committee room, a job, to mouth inanities; but the body has no value in itself.

We are immune to the world of Stettner. We hope he will go away as we hoped Miller, Bukowski, and a thousand other artists would go away. Many do; they go to Bomb School, inject heroin, drink themselves to death, join a guerrilla group in Peru. More often they go to Yale Law School, which goes on their resumes just underneath the MBA from Harvard at about the same time as their dicks and uteruses flop in the wind like freshly washed socks hung out to dry. "Long Dong Silver!" This cry goes up in school and marketplace, private office and public hallway, and its obscenity is matched only by another cry that brought us from the streets as children to congregate around the latest gadget in the snug bosom of our homes. This was the radio, and the cry was "Hi Ho, Silver!" Silver was the Lone Ranger's horse, and the Lone Ranger was a masked man who, aided by a dirty Indian who did all the dirty work, went around the frontier administering justice. No one ever saw his face, and he never hung around after his noble deeds to even accept a "Thank you, masked man." Except for Tonto, he was always alone and he dispensed silver bullets as his calling card. Henry Kissinger told reporter Oriana Fallaci in 1976 that he felt "like the Lone Ranger" when he was sneaking out of Washington at night to go to Paris to negotiate "peace" with the North Vietnamese. But who was Henry's Tonto? Us? Because if the Lone Ranger took Tonto behind a boulder at night and took off his mask, and there was genuine love between them, then everything's fine and I'm full of shit.

But if the Lone Ranger just fucked that Indian in the ass so he could shit silver bullets in the morning, then we're all fucked. There's nothing left to do but show each other pictures of chickens going down on strippers.

And if I seem demented in reducing the world to one great asshole, all you have to do is turn on the ABC's World News Tonight. According to Peter Jennings and two other reporters, sidewalk artists such as Stettner are not dead. No, not by any means. They vigorously survive on the coasts of Southern California and South Florida, where they charge $16 to $22 for a quick sketch of you...or you and your Tonto. There's one small catch. They won't draw your face...or even the front of you that might hint at the heart...or the genitals. No, you have to turn around, for these masters of the latest ideological vernacular are "Butt Artists." The ABC reporter made a big deal over "butt," persistently trying to egg the artists toward a more decorous name such as "rump" or "buns," but as one of the artists explained, "It is what it is and we call it 'butt'." Goodnight, wherever you are, holding your ass in your arms, asshole.

his own best friend:
on charles bukowski

Charles Bukowski mumbles better than other writers declare. Like W.C. Fields, his least movement, smallest utterance jars the prevailing quiet and order. He is an order unto himself and wherever he steps, whatever he reaches for, a dish falls, an old lady carrying a Bible is bumped, a merry-go-round of insanity is released. Though both men possess extraordinary physical coordination, they are also chronically absent-minded. Out of a paranoia about the motives of others, they hide money under the rug, under the ice-cube tray, in books, and then can't remember the next morning where they put it. Chaos ensues. They throw up their arms, they curse God and Walt Disney; they tear apart the house. Once, upon returning books to the library, Bukowski spotted something green peeking out of one book, and opened it to find three 20s and a 10-spot, a huge amount of money for him at any period in his life.

This absent-mindedness isn't for lack of concentration; Fields' and Bukowski's concentrations are simply elsewhere. They find the world odd, and beneath all the hijinks of their respective art forms, mostly loveless. There is little that endures and little that isn't pervasive quackery, and both men have a barely concealed loathing for the experts. What endures in their work is not so much any exalted notion of the primacy of the individual, but the pure difficulty of becoming and remaining W.C. Fields or Charles Bukowski.

Both men struggle prodigiously for some sort of equilibrium by trying quietly to locate an inner harmony, a small corner of the Earth where they can be left alone. They step out of the lonely claustrophobia of hotels and rooming houses to find a touch of human company in bars. Both have rotten nervous systems and alcohol is their sedative, and finally their poison. "Happiness," Fields once observed, "is quiet nerves." Both men pay a phenomenal price for burning off layers of false ego to get down to the essential nugget of personality unfettered by convention. Both artists have been battered as kids by Prussian-type fathers swearing allegiance to order, cleanliness, and a new refrigerator. Neither has ever had a sense of home except the inner cavities they created themselves: fantasies full of calamity brightened by their abiding sense of the ludicrous. This takes detachment and, for large chunks of time, a heroic separation from personal interest to gauge the nature of humans.

The problem is that the other bar patrons quickly pick up on this separateness. There is nothing like self-containment to arouse the suspicion of other human beings. As Bukowski once observed:

Not Wanting Solitude
Not Understanding Solitude
They Will Attempt to Destroy
Anything
That Differs
From Their Own

Black glances are fired their way. Silence invades the Perverse Pussy-cat Saloon. Knees jiggle against the bar fronting. "A stranger is among us," is the unanimous consensus. What to do with him?

"Where did you say you were from?" a regular might ask Fields.

"I didn't but as long as you mention it, I'm from Punxsutawney, Pa.," he says, dwelling lovingly on all of the syllables of ground-hog town, where he has never been.

"What brings you to town?"

"Nutmeg convention," Fields says proudly.

Soberly, the interrogator nods. Hostility is dissolved; men raise their glasses but there will remain a lingering bafflement at his presence, periodic glances his way.

The utter sobriety of patrons, even in a bar, is the point. It reduces them to a density and gullibility that's incredulous. It makes Fields and Bukowski chirp like a pair of canaries on a barbed-wire fence. People are constricted bags of barely animated features that release in the two artists a gaiety that dominates all of their work.

Like Fields, Bukowski is mostly a counterpuncher, though he has little of the comedian's hyperbole. The world isn't just ludicrous for Bukowski; it's half-maimed, and the flopping part of people that remains more or less alive is positively cannibalistic. Everywhere people are devouring each other and spitting out the indigestible remains.

In his movies, Fields shaves his truculent vision down to the absurd rituals of domestic and middle-class life with only a hint of the personal pique of poisonous residue of a society built on deceit. The world is all pomp and fraud and Fields punctures its balloon in one burlesque after another. An innocence akin to Dickens remains, and though men often admire someone like Fields who has a low opinion of humanity, the comic vision must be palatable: The bite should stay at the level of ha-ha. It shouldn't make people slow down and ponder their lives. That's per 20-minute short or 60-minute featurette. Yet, when you take the total accumulation of Fields' work, you realize he was playing it for a great deal more than the laughs. He distances himself from anything that might be called realistic and comes up with a truer picture of the U.S. than a hundred *Taxi Drivers* put together.

In thousands of short takes, poems, stories, Bukowski does the same.

At a glance, this work often appears as "slice of life" portraits of tawdriness and betrayal with a bizarre and deftly ironic twist. However, taken cumulatively, his 40 books produce a total picture. It is dark—people find ingenious ways of lopping off bits and pieces from each other and themselves—but it's finally as redeeming, invigorating, and, in these bludgeoned times, as necessary as fresh air.

If I have insisted on coupling two very disparate results, it's because Fields and Bukowski are two of a dozen of the truly unique U.S. voices of this century. Their lives and their work are instructional manuals on how to convert paranoia into galvanizing art. Manuals that can't be imitated. Fields and Bukowski eschew any sort of orthodoxy, not because they are rebels, but because they are so busy being themselves. Beyond their 50 feet of space, the world doesn't exist for them. They patrol that 50 feet with the vigilance of big cats, always with booze in hand. Fields hides in the bushes in the Hollywood hills, a bottle of gin in one hand, a highly erratic gun in the other, waiting for a mythical burglar who never appears. Twenty years later, a few miles below in an East Hollywood bungalow, Bukowski peeks out the blinds at any knock or strange noise in the street. He doesn't answer the door.

Both men make venturing out to the sidewalk a heroic

act. The streets are a disaster, and never for a second does either man doubt that there isn't someone waiting out there to do him in. Fields' specialty is dogs. They instinctively sense his separateness from the species that feeds them, and bound after him as if he were a rabbit. Most notable among Bukowski's pursuers are women of the type who shriek "Scratch his eyes out!" on Channel 50 wrestling. They have 3-inch-long fake fingernails and have applied their lipstick so ferociously that they appear to have been screaming all their lives.

A second type that Bukowski attracts might be called the "Literary Groupie." This creature, historically, has been well fed but resents it. They see in Bukowski's material deprivation the necessary ingredients for cooking up "poetic soul." They telephone him at 3 a.m., announcing in a theatrically hushed voice their admiration for his work and their willingness to drive to his place at that moment. "I read one poem and I knew you had soul. My husband's out of town. I think you'll like my poems." As much as a fourth of his output is devoted to getting rid of such women—after the itch of loneliness and gland has been sated. Sometimes they get rid of each other as happens in the poem "Who the Hell is Tom Jones?" An older woman enters his place to attack a younger rival while Bukowski's narrator surrogate sits, bemused and drunk, in his shorts. At one point he tries to separate them but he is 55 years old and no physical match for them; he wrenches his knee and retires to the bathroom to admire himself in the mirror and take a long-overdue shit. The two women shriek and claw and batter each other up the block. Squad cars arrive, as does a police helicopter. It was "better than the Watts riots," Bukowski announces. The poem ends with two cops leading the torn and blood-and-piss bespattered older woman into the bathroom where the cautiously joyful author sits on his throne. They "wanted to know why. /pulling up my shorts/ I tried to explain."

Though Bukowski will occasionally rant in full lyric rage, he is mostly the calm eye at the center of a hurricane. Especially in his later work, he parries the world with a deferential jab, feigning only modest interest in the latest enterprise foisted upon him. His opening lines often begin with a fake yawn. "Here we go again." This makes his pursuers lead with their heads which Bukowski continues to poke with a vaguely interested left. The men in his living room exhaust themselves, usually in confessions of failure, in an hour to an hour-and-a-half. In one poem he times their monologues.

But for the women he waits even longer. In life and in writing, his supreme virtue is patience, his favorite rejoinder, "Have another drink." Liquor reduces his ladies, and most everyone else, to a comatose state while culling in himself a calm resolve and a razor watchfulness. In a poem called "sticks and stones" Bukowski summarizes this resolve:

complaint is often the result of
an insufficient ability
to live within
the obvious restrictions of this
god damned cage.
complaint is a common deficiency
more prevalent than
hemorrhoids
and as these lady writers hurl their
spiked shoes
at me
wailing that
their poems will never be

on charles bukowski

promulgated
all that I can say to them
is
show me more leg
show me more ass—
that's all you (or I) have
while
it lasts

and for this common and obvious
truth
they screech at me: ·
MOTHERFUCKER.SEXIST
PIG!

as if that would stop the way the
fruit trees
drop their fruit
or the ocean brings in the coni
and the dead spores of the Grecian
Empire

but I feel no grief for being called
something
which
I am not;
in fact, it's enthralling, somehow,
like a good
back rub
on a frozen night
behind the ski lift at
Aspen

    The childhood chant of the title goes "sticks and stones
will break my bones but names will never hurt me." It's

part of his personal history that he's been called every derogatory name known, beginning with the repeated accusation of "FAILURE" from his father, and later echoed in a thousand rejections from women and editors because his face is ugly and his writing reflects an ugly world. Now in his 60th year (at the time of the poem), he has built his world and his armor against such accusations. The Bukowski world has always had an insistence on physical detail, especially if it can he related to the body. Our credos, ideologies, homespun decencies, in fact, most words fly out the window when presented with the body. He knows words become rationalizations for denying the body and eventually slaughtering it. The body doesn't want to be marched off to numbing jobs, calcifying marriages, frontline trenches; the body wants to march to bed. Mostly in bed (though occasionally at the track, or the classical music on the radio, or in a bottle) do the few bits of honesty, love, and beauty we still have within us rise to the surface.

It is in bed (with a bottle never far away) that the Myth of Bukowski is born, the myth minus its essential ingredients. From Tokyo to Munich to the queenly hallways of Vassar and back to Los Angeles, feature writers with douche bags for brains pump the myth of Macho Man. He is shown on the cover of this magazine and that feature section. To some extent, in letters and in public performance, he pumps this hype even as he rails against it in poems and stories. And even as magazine texts make the obligatory connection with Hemingway, "The Old Man and His Cock," there has never been a more unlikely subject for media hype than Bukowski.

Bukowski was writing for 30 years before the media came sniffing into the carefully arranged clutter of his living room. One time, early in the hype game, in trying to uphold the Macho Man Myth, his 55-year-old body rebels. Trying to screw a woman standing up, he throws his back out of place. Even before the first twinges ("the end of a short affair"), he is thinking "138 pounds, 138 pounds." After the woman leaves, the pain is so severe he drops a glass of water. He then places himself in a tub of hot water and epsom salts. The phone rings. With excruciating pain, he manages to extricate himself from the tub and reach the clamoring phone. It's the 138-pound woman.

" 'I LOVE YOU,' she said
'thanks,' I said '
is that all you've got to say '
'yes.'
'eat shit!' she said and
hung up.

love dries up, I thought
as I walked back to the
bathroom, even faster
than sperm. "

Thus, the court jester, the fool for all seasons pulls the string on this farce to guillotine the most dominant word of the 20th century. Love excuses the need to be sensitive or responsible, thoughtful or kind; each day almost as many murders are committed in the name of love as for country. Supply each person using the word "love" with a machine gun and soon the word love would equal the plagues of earlier centuries. It's not a matter of disparaging "love" per se; Bukowski longs for it periodically, searches for it like the rest of us, and occasionally finds it. It never lasts long and he doesn't blame anyone. The live ones—male or female—are clawing for some support system; the half-alive are propped on mannikin stands by little industries that are spurious and tyrannical in themselves. The world is a madhouse, and none of the schoolbooks or songs, *isms* or sects even attempt to prepare us to accept ourselves let alone the banal and carnivorous doings outside us.

What Bukowski has then, is what he has had all along, and what he always returns to—acceptance of his solitude. It is painful, and particularly in his early work he writes like a man hanging from a 20th-story ledge. But at least it allows him to have moments when he can see and hear in the mad juxtapositions of daily life what is really going on. Just as important, this solitude of his keeps him from becoming one of the "neutered faces glistening;" he gets to be that rarest of creatures—a personality not extinguished. He gets to be Bukowski.

I have written as if the seeing and hearing of daily life and the integrity of the personality reflecting in solitude are different things. They are not. At least not for Bukowski. Where other writers end, he begins. Most writers (or filmmakers for that matter) circle their material, hoping to extract a nugget of illumination, intimacy, true feeling from their subject. Bukowski's solitariness and gargantuan inner detachment won't allow him such conventionality. He's already up inside his material, looking out and at the same time outside, watching Bukowski trying to maneuver for his daily sustenance. It's the sort of daring that lands people in nut-houses, jails, or city morgues. The shock to our systems then, upon initially reading Bukowski, is the encounter with someone talking to us from the other side of the mirror. "Love dries up, faster than sperm." We smile with the shock of recognition. But what an awful thing to say, we think, what an overblown generalization. But even as we think such thoughts, we know we are reacting from habit, from the way we have been taught to think, the way that will continue our paychecks, the soft-soap job for our next piece of ass, the language of lies we hope will steer us toward somebody affectionate and lasting.

Bukowski will give us none of our habitual reflections. It is not through pronouncements he speaks to us. Not the screech of the rebel flailing out at the system, nor the beatnik heeding the call of the open road.

He has the luxury of speaking to us in a quiet, conversational voice because he is the insider, and we, with our accustomed comforts and our shopping cans full of lies and our pursed mouths ready to rage at some unlikely undeserving victim, are on the outside. Bukowski has walked away from the reflections that supposedly instill a sense of well-being to convert space into time and time into freedom. The work moves so leisurely; it ambles. Like Einstein, he seems unmoved by time. He takes the measure of everything so casually, yet so surely. He is in and out of the material in a few pages. It all seems so easy; how does he do it?

He does it so easily because he's back behind the mirror, inside the belly of terror. He tosses up bits and pieces of its body, and we smile or laugh out loud with recognition and say, "This guy's a bit much." It's not a matter of Bukowski describing terror and the night; he *is* the night, sinuous and not very approachable, his light-footed ambling a reminder of a self we forfeited long ago.

If I have rambled here at some length, it's because the vultures are circling the still-alive meat of Bukowski as they are doing with the bones of Henry Miller. The catalyst for combing the toejam of these men is of course a film, what else. Because schoolbooks are no longer the innocuous burblings they once were, and now are well-wrought clubs of oppression and repression, the citizenry is turned off books altogether by the age of 12. Also, the maniacal pace of life and people's capitulation to it have a lot to do with the ravings over the most sugar-pap films. A strong book requires the active participation of the reader. No less than the author, the reader must lay aside his social ego for a few hours to enter a new world. Not so with most films; a tether is floated to the exasperated mob, giving them an image to chortle over and try on the next day at the office, or that evening with the recalcitrant Wendy.

The movie that resulted in the Bukowski "renaissance" was 1987's *Barfly,* directed by Barbet Schroeder from a script by Bukowski and based on an early part of the author's life. I haven't seen it, but I do know it started the boys at editorial desks in several industries salivating. All hailed Bukowski for being "on the cutting edge of the dark side of the avant-garde," but what they were really hailing was their prescience on when to cash in the chips on yet another asshole who had the gall to think he could make a living writing from his gut.

As was the case with Miller, a New York commercial press that won't get near Bukowski's writing has seen fit to publish a biography about him.

"My first day on the job in a mass-market paperback house I had the distasteful job of being told to reject Charles Bukowski's *Notes of a Dirty Old Man* with a form letter," wrote the pseudonymous C.B. Coble in the January 1984 issue of the *American Book Review.* Coble, a commercial house editor who worked in a dozen publishing firms, concluded his rare blast from inside by saying, "What passes for publishing in essence has become lowest common denominator merchandising, with a few carefully 'controlled' deviations thrown in as a defense mechanism against meaningful criticism. Some will argue that publishing is a business. Granted. Everything is a business by 1983. And that includes the survival of basic values we once took to be self-evident."

But this is a little different than our daily lives where we rarely telephone another person unless we can use them. As Bukowski notes:

attrition rules
most give
way
leaving
empty spaces
where people should
be.
and now
as we ready to self-destruct
there is very little to
kill

It is not a matter of me fussing about systems—publishing or others; merely to walk down the street is a criminal act. We all should have been screaming from our rooftops the healing power of Bukowski, Miller, Giono, Himes, Fields, Keaton, Holiday, Bessie Smith, whoever, a long time ago. But...but the neighbors would have frowned. They would have heard us, gone inside, farted—and mistaken it for a mouse—and called the cops. Lip service to decency strangles us.

The author of *Hank: The Life of Charles Bukowski*, Neeli Cherkovski, is an awfully nice fellow, and in this book about his ol' buddy and one-time partner in a small-press venture, he pretty much loves everybody. Hank's (Bukowski's nickame) a success; his madness, his war with all that is mean and petty, his facial ravages from *acne vulgaris* have all been vindicated, and now here is Random House getting on the bandwagon, offering the final *Good Housekeeping* Seal of Approval for that mad dog Bukowski, at age 70 finally tethered to his kennel. So get out the beer and lintburger sandwiches, we're going to have a party, gang.

At first glance, Cherkovski avoids the travesty of a number of recent literary biographies, most notably those on Henry Miller. He doesn't seem to be bound and gagged to the pillar of respectable constipation that dominated the Mary V. Dearborn and Robert Ferguson books on Miller. Cherkovski is a poet and has been part of the West Coast literary scene for a long time. He is hugely sympathetic to Bukowski's work and the war the writer has gone through to produce his little time bombs. There are several good sections to this book, and yet on successive readings I always come away with the same feeling: Neeli Cherkovski is incapable of putting the Bukowski achievement into words.

On the surface, both the lively and dull parts of this biography present an interesting phenomenon: Where Cherkovski has men around on which to build his narrative—Bukowski himself; several small-press editors who launched Bukowski; John Martin, the author's longtime publisher at Black Sparrow Press; and *Barfly* director Barbet Schroeder—the writing has authority. It is crisp, and the content is relevant at a perfunctory level. But when he has to shift to the women in Bukowski's life, the energy flags; his heart skips first one beat, then two, then three; he loses interest; the prose deteriorates into one cliche or near cliche after another until it reads like a script for *As the World Turns*. "The loss of Jane [Bukowski's first love] darkened Hank's skies," he tells us.

Far more serious are those interludes where Cherkovski must take the stage—without the presence of Bukowski's backers—and address the nature of the author's work. To his credit, Cherkovski refuses to fall into the trap that Random House was expecting—the raunchy exploits of a beast that would rival the sleaze of the *National Enquirer,* all under the brand name of literary avant-garde. Periodically he keeps calling attention back to Bukowski's work and quoting chunks of it. Fine. But what does he make of it all? Is there any particular reason why we need Bukowski? Why read him?

If, as Schroeder correctly notes, Bukowski can't be identified with any outsider movements in literature, how is it that he surfaced at all through the clotted jungle vines of the herd-mentality, nit-picking, risk-disdaining, degenitalized literary scene of the United States? True, Cherkovski chronicles his publication history, but this doesn't explain why Bukowski's readings would draw 400 to 500 people in the '60s and '70s, when name poets would be lucky to attract half of that. Most of Bukowski's audience were involved in one or another of the protest groups of that era, yet he thought both public protest and groups a waste of time. "They got into the anti-war movement because they're lonely hearts," he told Cherkovski then. "They have no ideas of their own. These same people, if they were in control, would be just as bad as Johnson or Westmoreland." Then, what binds Bukowski's audience and his large readership to his writing, if at the social level he's so out of tune with them? And what was there about the '60s and '70s that nourished him into prominence?

It would be impossible for a Bukowski to emerge in 1991 and garner the following he mustered in the '60s and '70s. Yes, small presses with ambition, taste, and originality in their design spring up each month, but like their cousins at Random House, these publishers and their editors have all sworn allegiance to Junior

Scholastic in the seventh grade. The role then of John Martin at Black Sparrow Press is all the more important. Without John Martin there is no Bukowski. Where several previous small press publishers had located a readership of 400, Martin over a period of time got him 400,000 readers. About Martin, Cherkovski says, "Martin had already secured (by 1969) himself a permanent place in the history of American letters." Fine. But how? What obstacles to Bukowski did Martin overcome to get him nationwide distribution, publicity, or performing at such august colleges as the University of Michigan?

Among other questions not addressed are these:

Why does Bukowski receive the adulation of a rock star in several European countries, yet is still relatively anonymous in this country? Is it the media image of "the dirty old man," or do those German and Italian fans see his work as establishing an intimate relationship with their own aspirations? As Bukowski's German translator and promoter puts it: "Writers in his own country had a built-in censor, as though the spirits of the great classical writers were looking over their shoulders." But the U.S. isn't exactly loaded with uninhibited writers; writers here may not have "great classical writers" hovering over their shoulders but that hasn't kept their censors from being as "built-in" as anywhere else.

When Cherkovski does attempt to place the work and Bukowski in some sort of perspective, it reads like the prose-style of a jacket blurb writer at a New York publishing house: "Poems poured out of the great myth maker." "Bukowski's prose had the same kind of lean imagery as Henry Miller's. The sense of Whitmanic man prevailed, unattached to ideology...." "He became a patron saint for these wild young minds...." "He created a literary hand grenade to lob at the academy...." "He had not relented in his poetry, road maps for the man's daily sensibilities." "Jon and Gypsy Lou [early publishers] were survivors [emphasis added], like Hank himself." "I watched him move along with that Bogart stroll of his." "I guess the key to the secretive Bukowski lay in his gentleness, which he masked beneath a tough-guy exterior." And don't forget the Lone Ranger and his little girl, Tonto.

Cherkovski insists on coupling Bukowski with Whitman and Miller; at the same time, toward the end of the book he readily agrees with Schroeder that his work "had little to do with the Beat aesthetic, Henry Miller, or other 'outsider' movements in literature." If Cherkovski really believes this, why didn't he go back through his manuscript and qualify more carefully Bukowski's loose affinity with other breakthrough spirits, and then tackle the essence of the man? He does make brief headway in his interpretations of individual prose and poetry bits, but then quickly gets lost in more literary jargon talk, stuff like the "universality of man."

If this were simply a case of a well-meant but flawed biography, I would say, fuck it, and go lay in the sun. But there's something insidious here and it's this: Thoughtless adulation can cut the balls off a true voice just as handily as critical judgments spun to the latest sexual and political hysteria.

No sooner have I thought that thought than an idea even more grim shadows it. Neither Random House nor any other commercial publisher (and let me add 98 percent of the small and university presses) could have dealt with a manuscript that took the true measure of Bukowski. Cherkovski's insulated literary non-talk is acceptable to them, though the carnival barkers at Random House would have preferred something a little more scandalous.

I was reminded too of a conversation I had with one of Bukowski's German publishers some years ago at the annual German Book Fair on the island of Manhattan. When I asked this publisher why Bukowski's books weren't on display, he said, "My New York contacts in the industry think he's too crude. Of course, in California it's a different story."

His explanation is partially true; yet the affluent, whom those "New York contacts" sense, have their crudities and perversions like the rest of us. The difference is that the people who are willing to pay $27 for a book want their perversity clearly labeled "Serious Literature" on the bookshelves where the Trumps and Kissingers and the Goodeyganders can see it; and "pornography" at the back of the hall closet behind the china for special occasions.

Then, someone like Bukowski comes along and the "crude" is all mixed up with insights, for example this insight into what makes a woman a truly memorable human being: "There was something warm about her. She wasn't constantly thinking about being a woman." Or this insight into what makes a man dull: "Looking at my father I saw nothing but indecent dullness. Worse, he was even more afraid to fail than most others." An insight into language when writers like Hemingway use it: "Words weren't dull, words were things that could make your mind hum. If you read them and let yourself feel the magic, you could live without pain, with hope, no matter what happened to you." Hundreds of small insights attached to the rage of an acne-pitted 18-year-old trying to find some small corner of the world not dominated by "dull, trivial, and cowardly existence." This novel, *Ham on Rye*, written when Bukowski was 60, culminates its many wisdoms in a passage in the middle: "The problem was you had to keep choosing between one evil and another, and no matter what you chose, they sliced a little bit more of you, until there was nothing left. At the age of 25 most people were finished. A whole goddamned nation of assholes driving automobiles, eating, having babies, doing everything in the worst possible way, like voting for the presidential candidate who reminded them most of themselves."

No, the objection to Bukowski has little to do with the "crude." If such passages as I've just cited were taken seriously for a minute by the hardback-buying elite, the $25-a-plate sturgeon at Barney's wouldn't seem so appetizing, the $200-an-hour prostitute or wind-up dildo would lose its urgency. For a brief moment, the labels, by which the affluent and their minions the cultural arbiters wrack and stack the world so that their beef may be a bit more tender, their nooky more comely, their face lifts and breast implants and group sex protected under the watchful eyes of security guards at Sao Paulo, Bahamian, and Cancun hotels, are thrown into confusion, and they must wonder what it is to be a human being, what their brief lives on this earth have amounted to, if anything. If their children came across Bukowski's work, they would surely have a moment when they wondered whether to run away or blow Mom and Pop away while they slept in their $700 silk Bergdorf Goodman pajamas.

Such a moment cannot be allowed, will not be allowed.

The 38th-floor penthouses can shake, the president can shit oyster shells (or broccoli stumps) but we cannot have the supple, outraged, funny, utterly original voice of Bukowski among us. He has committed the grand felony of remaining himself and creating through 40 books a world that doesn't pay the faintest allegiance to anything we've ever been told about civilization.

A biographer who would have even attempted to get past the spurious labels by which the hardback-buying public carves up the earth and buggers it to a standstill, and reconstruct the comic-nightmare world of Bukowski, with all of its fits and starts, bravery and self-destruction and mock bravado, its anguish and small victories, its chronically precarious hold on life along with its insistence on not giving in to anything or anybody who is false—such a biographer would have been told in a form letter, "We wish you luck elsewhere." That's what they do up there in New York when you write something that is whole. They wish you luck. This is a euphemism and in reality is saying, "You asshole, don't you see how carved up the world is. Cunts and cocks and mouths and assholes on this side. Delicate and sensitive literary phrasing about the flawed but compassionate stature of man on the other side. Feel free to query us if you have a future manuscript that has a definite market in mind." Yes, darling, the butt-fuckers anonymous of East Orange, New Jersey.

For a biographer to have delved very deeply into the resistance toward Bukowski, to what John Rechy, writing in the *Los Angeles Times*, calls that begrudging of "respectful attention by the tomes that purport to establish literary importance," would have opened a can of maggots. It's not merely, then, that the New York "cultural elite," including Random House, would have been flushed into the open, but the whole gamut of "literary" houses, elite journals, and prestigious small-press publishers and magazines, wholesalers and distributors would have been set up like wooden ducks in a traveling carny to reveal them for what they are: just wood, and hollow wood at that. Then, once the prevailing and hopeless cultural hypocrisy had been sniffed out, the biographer would have been forced to go back to the work, to truly feel it, and evaluate it to see why Bukowski has so deeply disturbed all levels of the literary pecking order, indeed all of what can be called "respectable" society for the last 40 years.

He would see that much of the tension in Bukowski's work grows out of a fear and rage over the fly caught in the spider's web and the knowledge that life functions mostly in that way—eat or be eaten, Bukowski and all of us as murderers or murdered—unless, as Miller noted, humans can somehow find their way back to their custodial function as intermediaries between nature and the gods, preserving and enhancing what will grow, not die. That takes courage and imagination, and Bukowski has both. In the end it saves him from the vicious cycle of the treadmill that coughs up most people like battered tin cans.

And if the cultural scene is even half as calcified as I say it is, who would have benefited from a true biography of Charles Bukowski? It would benefit the 15- and 20-year-olds who feel lost right now, who in the words of Bukowski's fictional alter ego, Henry Chinaski, says, "Your parents controlled your growing-up period, they pissed all over you. Then, when you got ready to go out on your own, the others wanted to stick you in a uniform so you could get your ass shot off." These young people, at least a handful of them, also might be browsing the library shelves, as Bukowski once did, and perhaps remarking as Bukowski once remarked about books, "It seemed as if everybody was playing word tricks." Then...then to discover a book that speaks in true words about a true man and excites the bewildered 15- year-old to say of Bukowski's biographer, as Bukowski once said of John Fante, "And here, at last, was a man who was *not afraid of emotion.*" It won't happen, not in our lifetime, and probably never, no more than it happened for Gogol or Celine or Miller or Hamsun or Nathaniel West (W.C. Fields is an exception in having a biographer like Robert Lewis Taylor).

What we have is the work. It's all we ever have. And briefly, what might a 15-year-old think upon discovering Bukowski: Here was a man who found a way not to get hard like the others.

For Bukowski is finally Quasimodo locked in the bell tower of his alcoholic ding-dong, who, without leaving his room, rings the bells of alarm and saves beauty. No, not the beautiful woman, but the indisputable link between truth and beauty that resides in his heart, though he be labeled beast and his crossing the path of ordinary citizens be labeled "bad luck." "Oh that I were stone," Quasimodo cries, wrapped around a stone gargoyle as he watches the mob carry off the beautiful woman he has saved. But the beauty is that he, and Bukowski, haven't become embittered and turned to stone like the rest. As one anonymous and well-heeled coed cried to Bukowski after a reading at a fashionable Eastern college, "You're so ugly, you're beautiful."

masturbation in the strophe factory:
4 essays on contemporary poetry

(Author's Note: These essays were written in the early and middle 1980's. Little, if anything, has really changed since then.)

I

This article grew out of a letter sent to George Garrett. It was addressed to his remarks in a long article in the fall issue of The Texas Review *on the current rigor mortis of American Poetry. In the article, about 15 poets addressed Garrett's question: What would they like to see in my future poetry?*

When I first read Garrett I thought here's someone who has finally stuck a darning needle to that Great Blimp in the Combat Zone—American Poetry from 1960-1980. He and the poets interviewed simply said, "Let's cut the crap, start from scratch, be honest and write poetry that has a real need to be written." As I read each poet's comments on what he would like to see happen in American poetry, I readily agreed. The problem came after I had read them all: I couldn't remember one comment from the other. Now, this seems odd in a group as endowed with language and supposedly a desire for the truth as these poets are. Oh, I remembered a few scraps like "funkier language," "greater intensity, " "more mature," "closer to the heart," "greater plurality." But I didn't remember anything about the speaker or what he really wanted from poetry. If these poets were editors, would I have a sense of what their magazine was really about? Do I have any sense of them as people who eat, burp, fiddle with their nostril hairs, earn money, screw, and snooze? No, like most of the poems and stories being published, their remarks *seemed* modestly appropriate, modestly interesting, humane, covetously civilized.

No one said, "I'd like to read a poem that would make me laugh my ass off." Humor isn't mentioned at all among the 15 poets though Garrett does refer to "wit". No one said, "I'd like to see some poems with the jaundiced and high fallutin' spirits of W. C. Fields. I'd like to see a poem in the future which makes me want to trip my grandmother. I want some poems about snobbery and folly. I want poems that are infantile, prejudiced, ornery, set in memorable cadences that talk about how manipulation is bred in an American child since the age of two and how that child grows up to run an English department." No one said, "I'd like to see more poems like the kind I write." Well, I would—not the early poems but the kind I've written for the last four years.

A reader might not like the notion of meeting me in H.B. Springer Hall or climbing into the rack with me but dammit there's a hint of personality, a hint of temperament in my comments. And temperament is exactly what contemporary poetry and prose is lacking. The trouble with all the poets Garrett interviewed is that they wouldn't know what to do with "surprising" or "extreme" poetry if they got it. How do I know? Garrett, in discussing corruption in poetry awards, judiciously falls back on the statement, "In the real world we not only draw inferences from actions, we have to do so." Okay, I'll draw inferences from the poets Garrett interviewed and Hayden Carruth, poetry editor of *Harper's* magazine.

More than two years ago Carruth sounded the alarm, saying that a decade that began with so much poetry promise had fizzled into a terrible disappointment. His reasons and evaluations, like Garrett's, were mostly on the mark. Much as Garrett did, he took a hacksaw to what he called "workshop writing" spewing out of the colleges like cans of tuna. It took balls on Carruth's part to challenge the industry he was entrenched in and I told him so. I suggested some areas where he might dig the surgeon's scalpel a little deeper. Then I watched *Harper's*. What would they review? What kind of poems would they print?

Well, they reviewed slush and printed slush. Carruth reviewed Frances Mayes' book and Wendy Salinger's book, both of whom are as provocative as a whisk broom. Salinger won one of czar Halpern's National Poetry Competition awards and had been wormed into space on a New York publisher's list. Frances Mayes just happens to run the San Francisco Poetry Forum.

The above are examples of power responding to power. There were a dozen others. The same held true with the poems he's published between 1978-1980.

I challenged Carruth on the above and his response is interesting: "I'm willing to go along with your feeling that I failed . . . I write in a hurry, think in a hurry, and my comments about specific books may seem contradictory because I haven't worded them properly. I have thousands of manuscripts to read—I'm not joking—and that goes with starting a new semester in my new profession, plus an essay of 6000 words that was due on January 1 . . ."

Hayden Carruth, for all his relative honesty, good intentions, isn't going to change anything at *Harper's*.

And it's not because he's corrupt, not in the usual sense of the meaning of that word. He's caught in the numbers game. Like George Garrett and myself and most of the writers across America, he's running, running, running. Some are running for office. Most are just running because that's the nature of American society. If he were here to say to *Harper's,* "Look, this work load is absurd. Get some qualified readers and pay them well because poetry is psychological survival for me and might well be for a few hundred sane souls left out there," then Jimmy Ghost or whoever runs *Harper's* would say to him: "The magazine's on thin sledding. We're lucky to even run poetry. Be happy with what you have. You could be out selling insurance for a living."

A lot of writers have faced the same situation in universities or Poets In The Schools or any number of sponsoring agencies who play all kinds of games with us. The ten-year love affair the government had for American artists has come to an end. It was the kind of love a mother bestows on a child.

It isn't so much what they perpetrate on us as what we allowed to happen to us because we were scared we wouldn't get our cut. Compared to plumbers or lawyers or doctors there is nothing unusual there except writers were running around with a banner over their heads that said, "We got the Truth, Motherfucker." We got all decorous and respectable and self-conscious about our self-anointed priesthood. As I traveled the country harvesting my own cut of the pie (based on eight poems that were acceptable to arts council panels), I heard poets complain about ripoffs in the small press scene, chronic abuse and contract violations in PITS, and misuse of NEA funds for college readings and residencies.

Other than Jennifer Moyer, AIS coordinator of the Illinois Arts Council, who says the only way she could begin to rid the corruption festering in that state's arts council was to instigate open meetings which the press attended, I don't know of any writers or administrators who made much of a squawk about the wholesale slime that was connected with arts money in the '70s.

Poet David Ray has regularly run editorials decrying the lack of integrity of New York publishing houses. He is noted for his attempts to get PEN to set standards to protect writers. He prides himself on publishing the work of promising new writers. And he should. Once, though, he came up to me after a reading and said both my remarks and poems were "too confrontational." "That won't do you any good at all," he said. I replied that some of the poems had been printed in his magazine *New Letters*, but Ray shook his head as if shaking loose a fly on his eyebrow.

His message was much !ike that of a former arts coordinator : "You can pretty much do what you want in the classroom but be careful what kind of student writing you send to the newspaper." She was referring to fifth graders' poems about their umbilical cords that roused a Baptist School board out of their real estate offices for an "emergency meeting". The guest poet who perpetrated these umbilical atrocities—David Ray.

One could excuse the "image making" poets on the grounds that in difficult economic times they have to perform numerous and shoddy hustles just to eat and get a little writing done. Didn't Keats have to sneak up and down London alleys late at night snatching little doggies for medical experiments?

But there's a difference between "selling" the idea of poetry and strangling mutts. A casual remark from another "successful" poet (University of Illinois Press, *Paris Review, New Letters, Antioch Review)* does more to put the difference and the mediocrity of contemporary writing in perspective than all the NEA ripoffs and insidious "cronyism" over the past ten years. After reading two of my stories she said, "I could never write wild stories like this. Nobody would publish me if I did."

In a phrase she tells me what most writers have become: respectable. This explains why they don't buck those sponsoring institutions, why any gathering of them sounds more like probate lawyers hustling for corpses. Though 99.8% of the population wouldn't know Alan Dugan (a lot of poets don't either) or Russell Edson from the spring mechanism on an Atlas rocket, poets scramble and bicker over the fish bones of economics and power. Poets talk about their industry in the same spurious and soporific language doctors and lawyers use to conceal their billion dollar hustles.

When a poet does protest NEA shennanigans, the implications are ironic, if not grim. Take writer and small press editor, Dave Oliphant in Austin, Texas. Quite justifiably he, and others in Texas, complained that their presses were being short-changed while all the spoils went to New York and California (*The Texas Review* has a chart on this at the end of Garrett's article.) Under a barrage of angry letters and telephone calls, many of them Oliphant's, NEA whisked one of its representatives, former magazine editor Mary MacArthur on a plane to Austin where 400 of the faithful (a curiosity in itself since a poetry reading in Austin is lucky to get 50 people) waited in livid curiosity to find out why they weren't getting their cut of the pie. Lovely Mary, as might be expected, delivered a GM speech to the stockholders but many of the stockholders, including Oliphant, didn't buy it.

While Oliphant tried to badger Mary MacArthur out of her euphemisms, I couldn't help smiling. The previous spring I'd listened to Mr. Oliphant address students at the

University of Texas as part of an event called Small Presses of Texas Day or some such thing. A student asked: "When you're just starting out, how do you go about getting published?" Oliphant's answer: "You start your own press. You publish your friends. Later, when they get presses they publish you."

This is hardly a recommendation for me or the general public to buy his press's books or his own, especially when you consider that NEA and the Texas Circuit claim they're trying to promote contemporary literature. But Oliphant shouldn't be chided. He was only saying what is in fact going on in every state in this country. I've come to believe that any quality literature that does get published is largely by accident.

Groups forming to protect their identity and special interests are logical enough, except that literature used to be in the business of touching other people. NEA has spent several million dollars for "programs that would reach a wider audience" and that's money that might as well have been dumped in Grand Canyon for pack mules to munch on. As I've crisscrossed the country, I've talked to a lot of people who weren't writers, who've sampled one or two readings. A few were students; mostly they were people between 25 and 35; they struck me as bright, well-read in fields outside of literature, curious. A handful said they were delighted with the one or two readings they'd attended. The majority said they'd been bored and would not go back for another reading.

The most poignant remark of Garrett's piece is a writer's comment that poets are as much locked into the times as any salesman, doctor, lawyer, or Indian chief. Should we wonder, then, that if the times have become increasingly group centered and the members of each group increasingly monitored, that poets should have the same smugness, hypocrisy, respectability, and dullness as lawyers while offering us a product which, like our meat and soup, is increasingly watered down, loaded with artificials, and spiced with brilliant, vacuous labeling.

Where I differ from Carruth and Garrett and other writers about the literary scene is their contention that the mediocrity has been largely a product of university writing programs and grant giving programs. Garrett's analysis is far more complex, but I think the failure of the writing in the '60s and '70s goes much deeper. I do not share his optimism about the future of poetry or the poets he interviewed: "As much as each and all seem to be dissatisfied with the present situation, *all* feel that something can and ought to be done about it." (Italics mine.)

Much of my letter to Garrett discussed the above and for reasons of space can't be elaborated here. I don't believe writers are any more rotten than anybody else, just that all of us, particularly college graduates of any profession, have fallen for a tactic designed to keep us peaceful, law-abiding citizens: Discourse Mistaken For Reality.

It is something that began when we were in college and read our Orwell and Huxley and J.D. Salinger, railed righteously against the conformist world, and having found the right attitude, promptly went about the business of collecting the union card though it was dull, wearysome business day after day sitting passively in a classroom. Sixteen or eighteen or twenty years in school and not much to show for it except the *possibility* that we might eat a little better than our parents did and have a split level in Shaker Heights.

We have become a nation where the right things always get said but very little is done about it. The oil shortage hoax in '73 and '79, the Kennedy and King assassinations; the list is endless. The disease is one which spread from universities to the rest of the country—once having rigorously analyzed a problem, identified its roots, its possible remedies, we get smug and rest assured that problems will somehow take care of itself.

For many writers, particularly those who've laid a claim stake in the literary power system, the kibitizing and finger-pointing in the industry will suffice to restore a sense of moral rightness. To get off the train and quit running or being run may seem physically impossible to some writers because of commitments to raising a family. Others simply won't make the sacrifice. It would mean trying to find the tools and cultural supports to begin reshaping oneself. It would mean isolation and giving up the old cultural supports on which a false ego has been nurtured for so many years. It would mean undergoing the vertigo that the hero of Carpentier's *The Lost Steps* went through. It would mean loneliness that would drive weaker souls crazy.

A final anecdote. It's about the difficulty of maintaining a friendship with another poet when the other poet decides you're in the way of his literary survival. It's also about the incredible pettiness that characterizes relationships between writers these days. We'll call this fellow Rasputin. Aided by a priest, he slipped through some farm fields and escaped from Eastern Europe to the U.S. in the late fifties. We met as undergraduates over a sink as dishwashers in a college fraternity house. We had intense discussions about literature, collegiate conformity, the possibility that we might get laid next week or the week after. We lost track of each other for fifteen years but were reunited at a Sandra McPherson reading in Easton, Pennsylvania. Rasputin's got a shrewd peasant's sense of earthiness, loves a good joke, and is utterly unaffected. But . . . he decided to get into the small press business. He started a magazine. He took a poem of mine, held it for a year, then called me one Sunday to say he wasn't going to print it. It had the word "fag" in it, used ironically. Rasputin thought there was a certain member of the NEA grants for magazines panel who might object to the use of the word "fag". He had applied for a grant for the ailing magazine.

It wasn't just that I objected to a friend doing his hustle at my expense and a poem I had worked on for weeks to get right. It was more the feeling, "Oh no, not another one." Another one gone the way of a pettiness bordering on pathos where there was so little to be gained.

If ever there was a time when the lines from Yeats' poem made sense, it is now: *The best lack all conviction, while the worst are full of passionate intensity* .

II

Workers usually make the mistake of wanting to be regarded as respectable citizens, but no one thinks the better of them for it."
　　　　　　　　—B. Traven, *The Cottonpickers*

Poets for the last 30 years in America have not been much different than stockbrokers, psychologists, PR men, CPA's, suburban Methodist preachers, computer analysts, lawyers, doctors, and telephone company executives. Like their young urban professional counterparts, sometimes known as YUPPIES, their product is understood only by their own members; indeed, it was designed that way. The language between the doctor and the pharmacist is meant to be understood by nobody but themselves, though they do not drink the magic potion. It's the same with poets. Their jargon and non-talk insulates their elitism and protects them from scrutiny. True, they have few patients except a group of neurotic kids flocking to the writing programs but like other professionals they have been educated to mystify their work, to keep it tidy, obscure, and formal. George Garrett, in an article for *The Texas Review,* has said the more successful poets carry themselves "like priests."

Most lesser ones do it too. Their demeanor is grave, they seldom look healthy; the words are pronounced as if they were marbles rolling off a table. They are offering us ART. If the words rarely touch a nerve in us, a sense of recognition, that's because poets have become modest little technicians, not even relevant to themselves.

Here are some other traits shared by contemporary American poets and YUPPIES: a marvelous ability to reduce human conflict to comfortable, hollow notions; an utter lack of courage when confronting authority; little understanding or curiosity about America's role in world history; a curious deafness of tone; a detachment from their bodies both in person and in their work. The so-called professional poet is so sexless as to raise the question what he's doing on earth at all. Maxine Hong Kingston would have called them "ghosts." These ghosts scurry about with an air of self-importance, though any scrutiny reveals them to be ill at ease. They have little interest in a community except an intramural one that will further solidify their privileged position. The closer you get to the big cities, the higher you climb the professional ladder of success, the more you find a climate of "Every man for himself," a Darwinian orgy of sadism, self-flaggelation, and rigidity.

Poets view chicanery, manipulation, and duplicity as a way of life yet they are quick to condemn any act or person that strikes their specious morality as criminal. Violence is rejected, regardless of the situation, as a way of dealing with injustice. In short, you have in the American poet a person with the moral rigor of a Rotarian grain buyer, yet one whose evasiveness abets a society built on violence and hypocrisy. He is as institutionalized as a man who has spent his entire adult life in a maximum security prison.

Randall Jarrell's comment about how poets lost audiences and inherited classrooms after World War II is well-known. What is forgotten are the implications of the date: 1945. This is the year America began to move into the gap left by the depleted European nations and exploit the earth to supply luxuries a new middle class demanded. The process was very similar to Rome, systematically crushing the cultures of its neighbors which had for several centuries served as a buffer between the barbarians and the heart of the empire.

America was the barbarian after World War II. Unlike previous tyrants, it did not care if the Indian or Black man kissed the Cross (though Christianity could be useful in completing enslavement) or swore subservience to The Empire, or adopted the language of the masters. Much of the American Empire had already been built by slaves (black and white) and, unlike the French, it was seen as a disadvantage to have slaves around who could read or write. Anyway, America had only one culture to export and that was the desire for profit. It did not want the slave's soul, just his bauxite, oil, his fields bearing that one crop that Wall Street said would bring a good price that particular year.

1945 was the year the final brickwork of the old colonialism crumbled. As early as 1913, Ambassador Page had written to Woodrow Wilson: "The future of the world belongs to us. . . Now what are we going to do with the leadership of the world presently when it falls into our hands?" That "leadership," says Aime Cesaire, a poet from Martinique, not only mechanized man but completed "the gigantic rape of everything intimate."

As the Empire has grown and progressive wealth has been exported to America, the rich in the form of their foundation and museum lackeys, universities and arts councils have felt a greater and greater need to validate their exploitation. They want something called ART to prove they are "civilized" after all. This "Art" is the final dash of color, form, line, whatever technical jargon you want to use, to rationalize your room built upon skeletons.

There is no room for anything with real intimacy, content, boldness. It is too much for our senses which have been taught to see art as a subtle, civilizing maneuver. We do not need censorship; we censored ourselves long ago. The proof is this article. It will not excite any more comment, let alone action, than a man buttoning his fly at Times Square. In America everything is permitted and nothing taken seriously. In artsy circles it is considered bad manners to get excited about anything. Words themselves have become so inflated as to be little more than time-fillers till we find out who can be useful to our sad, little hustle. There is a feeling that all has been said, yet nothing came of it so it is not a matter of the rage in this article; rage and impotency are reflected in every other face on the street. A handful of people celebrate what there is to celebrate, which is still considerable—a young woman singing arias in a subway passage while the sultry mob surges around her, grim-faced as usual; a young go-getter in his Gimbel's wash n' wear suit and handsome briefcase raises his index finger to his temple and makes the screwball sign. Our poets will not be witness to any of this, not the breakdown, nor the joy of the courageous few.

It's not that I would have them go to El Salvador via Carolyn Forché and detail the bodies in the town dump. Forché's poems on that country are affected, condescending little set pieces and show what happens when an American poet tries to overlay his education in technical subtleties with an atrocity. You get a crash course in slumming.

No, I would have poets take seriously what Baudelaire wrote: "Everything in this world reeks of crime: the newspaper, the wall, the countenance of man."

By knowing what to say "No" to, they could then discover those eyes, hands, artichokes, cafes, loins, and screwdrivers that deserve their resounding "Yes." It is precisely American poets' inability to identify the enemy that makes their poetry so mediocre. Instead, they have worn the mantle of the outsider, the priest, the defeated without realizing that writing is a privilege taken mainly by stealth; and, in the words of Victor Serge, "no one is ever really outside society." The notion of the suffering poet in his garret is little more than a romantic myth perpetuated by art's hucksters. The bourgeoisie love that mythology as long as they don't have to get too close to the messiness of art. Poets have cooperated in recent years by cleaning up their act, by being respectable little citizens as they paraded to the podium, yet hinting that their wares came from untold privation and suffering. Such "artists" have a literary ego but no real ego and anybody with true well-being, any real gusto for life, will by virtue of his mere appearance among them find himself singled out as The Enemy.

Balzac and Stendahl, among others, have detailed the process of the above paragraph. In *Lost Illusions,* Balzac has Lousteau tell the budding poet Lucien, "The key to success in literature is not to work oneself but to exploit other's work. . .The more mediocre a man is, the sooner he arrives at success; he can swallow insults, put up with anything, flatter the mean and petty passions of the literary sultans. . . "

Luis Bunuél put American literary history in perspective when he said, "It seems clear to me that without the enormous influence of the canon of American culture, Steinbeck would be unknown, as would Dos Passos and Hemingway. If they'd been born in Paraguay or Turkey, no one would ever have read them, which suggests the alarming fact that the greatness of a writer is in direct proportion to the power of his country. Galdos, for instance, is often as remarkable as Dostoevsky, but who outside Spain ever reads him?"

It is not merely the power of a given country but to what uses they can put foreign writers. Solzhenitsyn is given large press but who knows that the contemporary Voinovich is an infinitely better writer? Or for that matter other Soviet writers who were not officially sanctioned in the old USSR—Alexander Herzen; Vissarion Belinsky, whose literary criticism if taken seriously by American critics would result in a whole new look at our writing; Victor Serge, political historian and novelist.

The Peruvian poet Vallejo's work was well-known by Spanish and European poets in the 30's. Why did it take 40 years before his brilliant, sombre poems reached American poets?

Why in the recent "boom" of Latin American writers is the Cuban novelist Alejo Carpentier seldom mentioned except by Hispanic writers?

The list could go on and on about a body of writing with a greater variety and feeling for the truth than American culture offers. I am forced to conclude that Bunuel is right: American books are found throughout the world, not because they are the best that can be offered, or are even good, but because it's a dying Empire's abortive effort to prove that it is, after all, civilized.

The Mailer's, Updike's, Bellow's do not challenge the systems which give them their preeminence. They are held up as cultural ideals but their work has no center of feeling or thought and more important, little sense of surprise. Typical of American writing, these esteemed artists muddle in a moral anarchy rather than clarifying it. In interviews they would make us think otherwise but their own writing, for all its dabbling in ideas, finally reinforces the American cultural norm: there are no ideas worth taking seriously.

Despite the fact that one-half the population has gone to college, where they all get at least a semester of exposure to literature, most Americans still think of serious writing in the context of "ivory tower", "romantic", "effete", and above all, Intellectual. These terms may be unjust, given a certain variety in American fiction and poetry during the last 40 years, but they have a very real basis. The tradition of fiction and poetry in most of the world, particularly outside Western Europe, has not only cast deep suspicion on the powerful and rich but reveals a consistent interest in the lives of the marginal, the oppressed, the mad, the eccentric, the poor. Except in America. John Kenneth Galbraith's comment about our best writers' attitude toward the rich summarizes fiction but the inferences drawn from it can easily be applied to poets: "In the late 1920's and the years of the great flowering of American fiction there was a major change in the treatment of the rich: they ceased to be socially offensive or economically exploitive and became positively benign. Now it was *their* problems that attracted attention. This, perhaps surprisingly, continued to be true in the Depression years of the 30's, 'The Grapes of Wrath' being something of an exception, as also the earlier novels of John Dos Passos."

How interesting that this comment comes from someone outside the literary camp.

The term "rich" is bound tight with another word, "respectability." In a country where there has not been the cultural and historical division of classes as there has been in other countries, writers have often shopped in both camps of the rich and the marginal, using language both respectable (tactful they might say) and blunt. Mark Twain-Samuel Clemens may have originated American vernacular but he also started the "business" of the artist cowtailing to respectability when he allowed his wife to delete any words she thought offensive in *Huckleberry Finn*. His schizophrenia of wanting to play ball in two opposed camps is at the heart of American writers' ultimate loneliness and desperation. I've always found it amusing that Twain is held up as an example of a satirist.

Even more amusing in the last twenty years is the obsession of American poets, bordering on a mania, for respectability. Since no one is listening to them, not the government, nor any audience even approaching an intellectual body, nor the literate masses, I find this mania pathetically comic. I can think of no more deluded or sadder group in this country.

Both writers and audiences began at the same place: until the age of two we were taught to walk and talk; after the age of two we were told to shut up and sit down. Fifty years later, most Americans are still sitting down and shutting up. This is what makes a "great" technological power able to exercise political power in Chile, economic power in Central America, dominance over seven tenths of the world. Indeed, the former slave countries of Ireland and St. Lucia in the West Indies, for all their misery, strike me as considerably freer in their expression than this dominant country of technocrats.

I think of part of the definition of a poet as someone who feels more deeply and sees more clearly so as to be able to show his country how to see more clearly. To do this he would have to rebel at some point against this shut up and sit down dictum. Judging by most of the poetry written, such rebellion has never taken place. They have been busy being "good" little boys and girls. A more honest profession would have been as pimps at 23rd and 10th in New York. But the illusion that they are professionals in "art" persists, and the arts councils and universities aid them in this myopia.

Eight years ago Edward Albee told a Bucknell University audience, "You people don't want the truth; you just want to be entertained." The repressive backlash from the 60's gets more constraining each year on university campuses. Yet they continue to make room for more poets, more workshops, more conferences. Poets cooperate in this relatively new business hustle by essentially being passive. If they told those middle-class twits, not sure what to do with their lives, the truth, the kids would take up data processing. But the poet, himself, long ago has learned the same game his students have—SHUT UP AND SIT DOWN. As he gets older, our poet learns that the rules don't change, just the title for them. He must wait for authority before he marches to recess. He must pare his wildness, enthusiasm, anger, sense of misgiving, sadness to manageable proportions. Above all he must learn the lesson so obvious at every level of American society—people don't count, just your superiors. Much of this our little poet has learned by junior high school. Only now it is called DON'T MAKE A MISTAKE.

"You make one mistake and you're out," is what an arts administrator told me when I went to Texas in 1977 to do poetry-in-the-schools work. She liked the idea of kids getting "art" and her own notion of art was largely taken from Bach and medieval art. I doubt she was aware of Benvenuto Cellini and the absolute war it took to produce "pretty" vases; in other words her idea was that art should be "decorative". This woman is a distinct and recurring type found in arts bureaucracies and the type is not there by accident. Like our Yuppies, the poet and his pal, the arts administrator, all hold hands down a primrose path strewn with pleasant diversion. Struggle must be eliminated if the machine gears are to roll smoothly and those who insist on any sort of struggle are violating DON'T MAKE A MISTAKE.

Naomi Lazzard made a mistake even considering doing an article commissioned by Harper's on "the poetry mafia," a comical misnomer in itself. Carolyn Kizer told her so; so did "a number of other prominent poets." They told her she'd "be finished in poetry," if she did such an article. Various arts councils and universities pooled their resources and bought her a bottle of liquid soap and as of this writing she is blowing bubbles in various MFA programs around the country. Everyone considers her a success. To be a success is to be respectable. Wherever you are reading this, stand up and applaud the success of Naomi and Carolyn and wee Richie Howard and Uncle Kunitz and all the other poet successes quietly sitting at the front of Mrs. Diefenbacher's fifth grade class, quietly polishing their apples.

Those writers who do not go along with the party line get fired, and sometimes so do their friends. It goes on all the time in the American Yuppie scene and in economic terms it's called "carom screwing". The ironies pile over each other with the speed of a Marx brothers movie. The demand for instant success insists on a language that is both specious and cautious. Everyone, everyone must obey the party line. But in a theoretical democracy, no one is quite sure what the party line is, so the scramble becomes more and more insane each year. A single poem can have four or five contradictory messages. Yes, there is an easy workshop writing going on, born of casual metaphor but poets' failure to find out what they really feel and think makes them subject themselves to psychotic splits and we get a poetry utterly without clarity. Their struggle is not a real struggle; their voices are those of men and women who write out of habit but no conviction. Some editors complain of the lack of humor in poets but that's because they have never struggled for anything beyond success. Mayakovsky committed suicide after writing poems for the new-line Bolshevik regime which squashed all freedom in Russia. American poets don't have that kind of courage; they commit a slow suicide because unwittingly they speak in the interests of repression. They hark back to Whitman and Eliot but show me one that even approaches Whitman's buoyancy or Eliot's critical powers. Poetry in the states operates in a vacuum where history is discarded and poets become the sycophantic clerks their fathers were.

III

"The mere fact that the younger American literary generation has come to the schools instead of running away from them is an indication of a soberer and less coltish spirit."

—Wallace Stegner, Stanford University,
Creative Writing Program

W. D. Snodgrass, in his foreword to *Dance Script with Electric Ballerina by* Alice Fulton, the Associated Writing Programs' award co-winner this year in poetry, explains a disease which has run rampant for so long it now feels ancient, not merely with AWP, but with other prizes as well: "On every side manuscripts appear, with high praise, exactly like seven other volumes one has read that year; if you accidentally dropped and scrambled all eight manuscripts, not even the authors could tell. In place of real talent, energy, passion, one sees poem after poem" (or story after story) "written to fit the fashion, the political or literary movement of the week, the needs of 1,000 half-dead graduate students, the obsession and power-hungry theories of critic A or B."

Like other able critics of the shriveled literary spirit in recent years, Mr. Snodgrass sees clearly the symptoms but not that he and a few thousand other writing teachers are part of the cause. If he were to say to those "half-dead graduate students" who show up in classes, "You're half-dead because you've been hanging around school for the last 17 years. The first assignment in this course will be to get out of here and take a job as a checkout clerk at Woolworth's," Mr. Snodgrass would be thrown out of his warm stall and forced to join his creative writing majors at the five-and-dime, or the unemployment line.

AWP is AWP because creative writing programs have blossomed ten-fold in the last thirteen years and this could not have happened if more than a thimble's worth of critical spirit or life had seeped into the classroom. It's so much easier to do metaphor exercises, character sketches, and study line breaks than talk about the expansiveness of James Wright or Whitman or why Robert Penn Warren makes the statement, "there's a lot of talent out there but not much fire." Students are satisfied they're getting something tangible; their basic sense of comfort hasn't been tampered with. As long as you're locked in "workshop exercises" everyone has hope and pays their money for the next term. The writing teacher hasn't said anything controversial or defeating; the deans haven't had to deal with anything messier than a writing instructor screwing an occasional student; the English Department chairman is satisfied something like "real discipline" and not "a bull session" is going on in your classroom. At the AWP convention in San Antonio in 1980 I listened to several writing teachers whine about the "prize-winning" poems and stories that had just been read by the proud authors. But none of them whined where it could be heard. It would have been bad for business.

Umberto Eco, touring America this year, compared humanities departments to prisons. They have no relationship with the community. This would be unthinkable in Italy, he said. When you add to this claustrophobia the pettiness and hypocrisy of the American university, is it any surprise that its products have as much relevance to people's struggles as a pound of oleomargarine? But the creative writing boys such as Mr. Snodgrass would have us see them as mavericks within the system.

If the young writer needs an instructive example of the meanness and pettiness and utter disregard for talent with which many universities treat the writer who tries to go his own way, he could do no better than a biography on Theodore Roethke called *The Glass House*. Can anyone imagine an American university printing a Gorki, Nathaniel West, Rabelais, or Nelson Algren?

What we have as a fiction prize-winner is *Delta Q* , by Alvin Greenberg. The collection was chosen by Ted Solotaroff from approximately 200 submissions. Solotaroff is an editor of "serious" fiction at Harper &

Row and his choice tells us something about the diminishing distance between large and small presses. Solotaroff does not offer us a Foreword explaining his selection but if the title and rarified tone of the stories bewilder us, the back cover offers us enlightenment: "Just as the Heisenberg Uncertainty Principle, from which the title is drawn, postulates a limit to the accuracy with which science can observe and describe the universe, so Greenberg examines man's perplexity at the discovery that human knowledge is limited."

Greenberg's first examination centers around some pigs. Their lead sow scratches the word LOVE in the dirt. This leads the nameless narrator, a writer—what else—to some ruminations about what pigs have done to a library: "Whole books, my own among them, are missing. I am not sure how to account for this, but it makes little difference; there is enough reading material here to last a lifetime, and besides, are we not now in the very process of developing an entire community of writers on this island? Soon, soon, I hope I will be able to begin reading them."

Mr. Greenberg will have access to them sooner than he thinks because as he knows they are *group*, and as *group* they will be quick to imitate the nation's prize winners, including Mr. Greenberg.

Greenberg's stories feed solely on interpretation; the dissertation folks at MLA would have a field day with them. Many of them are monologues by narrators without names, without a neighborhood, without an odor, with the energy of a sloth just after feeding time. What they do offer is a muted, cautious irony like a blinking yellow light to remind us life is a remote snicker. This irony is about so little that I finally suspect that the joke is on Greenberg. He doesn't have very much to write about except writing and literature, as the following titles indicate: "The Power of Language," "To Be or Not to Be,""Disorder and Belated Sorrow," "Not a Story by Isaac Bashevis Singer," "Who Is This Man and What Is He Doing in My Life?" Should The Club members complain this year about the quality of the prize winners, Greenberg can tell them, "Some pigs are more equal than others."

In citing the virtues of Alice Fulton's award-winning book, Snodgrass says, "Her life seems to have been a succession of dances, dancers, performers, costume." I wouldn't quarrel with this. There is great color, movement, and dazzlement in this poetry. Almost every line is a blazing light show. That is the way Fulton would have it: "You've seen kids on Independence Day, waving/sparklers to sketch their initials on the night?/ Just so, I'd like to leave a residue/ of slash and glide, a trace/ form on the riled air."

But sparklers fizzle very quickly; to keep up the illusion that something real is going on, you have to light them faster and faster to convince the crowd this day was worth celebrating. The search for independence gets lost in the fireworks display.

In discussing her own buoyancy, Ms. Fulton says, "I didn't create this painful grace./ I didn't banish the primitive." After reading these poems several times I feel this is exactly what she has done. She is so conscious of the clever turn of phrase that she consistently out-finesses her subject. The primitive has been banished; there is a grace to these poems; but it is not of the "painful" variety.

About her tendency to out-finesse her subject, Snodgrass says, "It may be that at times the fancy footwork obscures the overall shape of the dance—which is to say, I suppose, that she has not quite decided whether she is a poet of style, like Cummings or

Berryman, or a poet of subject, like Hardy or Frost."

Such subdivisions by Snodgrass are a lot of nonsense and go a long way toward explaining why we have several hundred cute poets getting prizes for stringing together snazzy images. It explains why 90 percent of the poetry today is inaccessible to anybody but other poets. Style grows out of character and character is our response to the pressures of life. You can relay those pressures in a light manner or a solemn manner or any combination of the two but if you're not deeply involved with your subject matter you get sparkler writing on the air. In citing Pound, Snodgrass calls it "the dance of the intellect" to describe Ms. Fulton's work.

This "dance of the intellect" looks to me like a lot of running in place. There is the illusion of motion but no real movement except in three or four poems where the writer lets other people speak. I have no more sense of knowing the poet here than I would a man running for comptroller with whom I'd spent three hours. Language as a smokescreen. Perhaps this is what Snodgrass means by "the dance of the intellect."

The proliferation of the mediocre is not really news. Imitative dullness, cowardliness, modest aspiration, and lack of a real voice have dominated the daily skirmishes of most literary ages. Balzac documented the literary scene in 1820 in France; Orwell alluded to its corruption often in essays, letters, and book reviews. What is fascinating is the process by which mediocrity gets called art, be it Raymond Carver or in this case some university award winners. In Balzac's time, if a reviewer wanted to pan a book he said "it is the finest the period has produced." That was said about all books, language inflated to say nothing at all. Now we resort to euphemisms that actually amount to an "intellectual dance."

105

As to why we are offered so much colored dish water that's labeled DRINKABLE, Pablo Neruda says it best: "The bourgeoisie demands a poetry that is more and more isolated from reality. The poet who knows how to call a spade a space is dangerous to capitalism on its last legs." Capitalism, or Socialism for the Rich, the point is that poems should match the handsome bookcases full of culture which we all know begins with a hush. By its harshness or playfulness, celebration or disdain, a book of poems or stories must not jar the prevailing quiet of the isntitution that sponsors it. The result is Understatement as a Fetish by Spanky and Our Gang.

When a writer does choose to do a little spade-calling, the process of voluntary censorship to which they allude is fascinating for its implications. In 1981 *Poets & Writers* interviewed Naomi Lazard on a subject called the "poetry mafia." Ms. Lazard said she'd been asked by Harper's to do an article about the "potry mafia." "She wanted very much to do it," the article says. " 'I was told by several people—including Carolyn Kizer—that if I did it, I'd be "finished" in poetry.'" It's irrelevant whether there's some lyric rhapsodizers toting bean shooters labeled "a poetry mafia"; the attitude of sycophancy and knuckling under make "the family" unnecessary. The knowing Ms. Kizer labeled John "The Whisperer" Ashbery and Harold "Two Knuckles" Bloom as some of the leaders of this "mafia," which shows how little it takes to make the literary crowd tinkle in their boots.

The reward for being a quiet little poet, according to Kizer, is "power" which is "who gets listened to and who doesn't." Since 90 percent of the audience is centered around colleges, poets are fighting over a podium in front of fifty metaphor-logged creative writing students, a glass of sherry, and a chance to admire the dean's wife's new henna hairdo. The lesser colleges offer the visiting writer the chemistry room where he can spot the foreheads of his audience just over the top of the bunsen burners. Then, if your writing is judged harmless enough for five consecutive years, you get a two-week paid vacation at the Bread Loaf Writers' Conference where, as Gene Lyons reported for *Harper's*, a Vietnam veteran reading from his war experiences was enough to make the veterans of quietude scamper from the carpeted room, mumbling, "Taste! What's become of taste!"

This quietude is what *The New York Times* called "the agony and ecstasy at what is generally considered the best author's course in the United States—the Iowa University Writer's Workshop." Iowa was not only in on the ground floor of writing programs but of a university prize (actually furnished by the Iowa Arts Council, which is an amazing entity itself) for short stories, presumably like these AWP prizes, making up for the New York publishing houses' lack of interest in the short story or serious writing in general. They were so serious about this prize one year in the mid-70s, they hired a writer who we shall call Jameson to screen almost three-hundred short story manuscripts by himself. They gave him a thousand dollars and three months to boil these submissions down to twenty finalists. Jameson's job was not made easier by the fact that he isn't American. He's from New Zealand and this was his first visit to the States. What he would have done with the idiom of a Richard Wright or a Flannery O'Connor I don't know. But Jameson had his own idiosyncratic approach to such servitude. If the type on the first page was light, he threw it in the rejected pile, he later told me. If the first page of the first story didn't engage him, that manuscript too plopped with the rejects. His advice to me: "If you ever submit to the Iowa contest, buy a new typewriter ribbon first."

william joyce

My information is that last year's Walt Whitman contest (Academy of American Poets) did employ three screeners to handle several hundred poetry manuscripts. Two of them were MFA students; the third was a young man who said he needed a job. Eric Staley, head of AWP, assures me that for his contests there were four screeners, "each with a published book." However many, it may not be enough to assuage the prevailing feeling among writers that these contests aren't much more than a lottery system. The sponsors no doubt would say there just isn't enough money to pay strong screeners, yet it is curious how universities can always come up with a spare thousand when a "star" writer calls for a reading. Finally, if the two books reviewed here are even among the best, it may not matter how many screeners contests employ or how much they pay them, and writers would be better off investing their time, entry fees, and postage on the weekly lotto.

So why is the postman burdened each week of each year with thousands of manuscripts if writers are fed up with the system? "The only way to get any attention is to win a prize," Greg Kuzma, a Nebraska poet, advises me. Each year, then, we have more and more writers listening to teachers they don't believe, submitting to contests they don't believe in, all so the magic ball with their number on it will be plucked from the wire cage and they will be able to coast for a few years, passing judgment on students and getting paid for it.

Even the normally soft, and sometimes downright sycophantic, *New York Times Book Review* is getting hip to the dreariness of it all. Says David Bromwich (of Princeton) about W. S. Merwin's latest book, "Mr. Merwin has all the equipment of a poet, but for the moment appears to write from habit rather than impulse...." This phrase could describe 90 percent of the poetry and 70 percent of the so-called "serious" fiction published within the last ten years. And Merwin is one of the "stars" who wander in and out of classrooms, advising students.

Heads of creative writing programs are reluctant to tamper with this "star" system even though their students would get more for their money if the head would take the time to find out which writers can write and which writers bring imagination and critical penetration to a workshop. As one writing head explained to me, "No one comes to a reading if the writer's unknown." At the same time, the "stars" know they have nothing to lose by a sodden performance; it will not affect future bookings.

In 1971, the University of West Virginia hired Norman Mailer to spend two hours with its students at a cost of $3,800. For an hour and forty-five minutes of that time, Mailer showed two of his movies and they were dull indeed. When I complained to Mailer by letter saying students deserved better for their money, he wrote back a generous letter, apologizing and explaining that he had been behind in his alimony payments and had to give ten appearances in nine days. This attitude isn't exceptional. Judging by the quality of their readings or addresses, most stars know the university is an easy udder to milk. But the faculty committees and writing programs will go on playing the game because they know damn well the rules of the game do not include the student voice. They are on safe ground—much of the time students are happy to have glimpsed a star whether he has said anything arresting or not.

If this were just a little game played out in colleges, it wouldn't be worth my time addressing. But when you consider that most students arrive at college hating both writing and any reading which challenges their preconceptions, the situation is hypocritical and pathetic.

The university is the one institution capable of reversing the situation before young people get funneled into society. Yet its writing programs at every level echo the dreariness and rigidity of the American public school, for reasons just touched on here.

According to Ed Ochester, head of the creative writing program at Pitt, as well as overseer of the Drue Heinz Prize, the Agnes Starrett Lynch Award (for a first book of poetry), and the University of Pittsburgh Press, a committee of faculty and deans must approve visiting writers. Their criteria: 1. the writer must not be politically controversial nor be likely to read politically volatile work; 2. the writer should not be likely to try and seduce faculty wives or students. I don't think Pitt is unusual in this respect.

In discussing university writing programs, Nelson Algren once wrote, "A dedication to the printed word may conceal an indifference toward cruelty; and that understanding of justice and human dignity becomes enfeebled in proportion to one's sophistication should be obvious by now. Unless we've forgotten that it was scholars well-disciplined in Shakespeare, Hegel, Goethe, Freud, Marx, Dante, and Darwin, who yet devised the cultural programs at Auschwitz."

I have my own small experience with a university's obliviousness to injustice or cruelty. Two-and-a-half years ago I wrote to Eric Staley, then editor of the *Missouri Review*, now head of AWP, proposing an essay which dealt with what I considered low-handed tactics by the Missouri Arts Council on writers it sent to schools. His response: "The current genre divisions of the magazine, however, do not seem appropriate to such an essay (they are poetry, fiction, literary criticism, interview, omnibus review). I think the situation is such that the staff would 'worry' about that one when it came up." It used to be called "Protecting my ass," but rarely do you get one of the literary fellas to admit as much. So on top of all this erudite nonsense you get an industry that's stone humorless.

I often associate the word "writer" with "complaining" and most of the complaints listed in this review I've heard from writers at one time or another. But they complain among themselves, never to the appropriate sponsor. As to why this happens, Algren, from the previously quoted essay (which no magazine would print), is best qualified to speak: "Writers bespeak a readiness to be cowed in return for a stall in the Establishment Barn; at whatever cost of originality. They will not buck. They will not roar. At times they may whimper a bit, softly and just to themselves; but even that they will do quietly."

As visiting writer to the Rocky Mountain Writers Conference in 1968, Algren bombarded his students with water balloons from the roof of his motel. If creative writing programs have to go on, I can think of no better way to begin a class. A truly ambitious program would follow up on this. It would schedule writing classes in a shower room and turn the water on full blast. True, the ink would run but our society is short of competent plumbers, electricians, roofing installers, and auto mechanics.

IV

With hysteria bubbling over about restrictions on the National Endowment for the Arts for 1990-91, perhaps writers will now sit down and take a good look at their own institutions including magazines and reading series, reviewing and trade magazines, prize granting, bookstores—the whole damned lot. From top to bottom, from McMurtry and Keillor (defenders of NEA) to those still unpublished writers, I want them to ask themselves one question: How have we censored ourselves? Until they ask this question, writers are just little urchins standing alongside the road with their hands out, waiting for a sugar-daddy to round them into shape.

From 1972 until 1985 I worked in all sorts of writerly programs, many of them funded by NEA. I am grateful for the chance to have observed how art for thousands of children was not just a bland goodie dumped on them after geography class and just before football practice, but part of their joyous, surging bone marrow.

My God, the stuff they wrote—elated, terrible, funny, sad, and unpredictable. They changed not just the way I thought about writing but about life: We are all born to create; it is that simple and if we don't create, we die. At night, during formally arranged meetings of the PTA, or informally in restaurants and bars, I met these kids' parents and passed out copies of that day's work, and the parents instinctively understood that something valuable was going on. It was a little better to work in the Midwest and Southwest and Plains States than the two coasts, but on the whole, dozens of community organizations gave rich support to children's art.

But a poison was seeping in, surreptitiously at first. Now it is blatant and open. Jesse Helms (who wanted to eliminate the NEA) and we artists of the United States deserve each other. We are much closer than any of you have even begun to guess.

To put the whole business in statistical perspective, arts administration was the second fastest-growing curriculum (next to business administration) in the U.S. during the 70's. From the NEA's inception in 1967 up until 1976, there was a real pioneering spirit because arts programs, like Czechoslovakia in 1990, was run by amateurs. The term "professional writer" reared its head about the same time the phrase "professional arts administrator" seeped in..

The very popularity of arts programs made the administrator and the artist see that art could be used for all sorts of ends that had nothing to do with creation itself. The right image could create a constituency, and in a very young country (as Mr. McMurtry has noted), still fumbling for a moral and cultural base, only a constituency could ensure survival.

There were numerous able arts administrators but usually they were fired by states' arts councils for "not sufficiently promoting arts programs." Like all aspects of today's American society, art was not allowed to progress at its own pace. It had to be pumped, perpetually inflated, constantly sold to some dubious community down the road, always with the right image in mind. It was bonanza time once again at John Sutter's mill, and now we are choking on the poisonous residue of that mineral processing.

Caution and safety were the passwords to artistic success in the '80's. Gold is not what you make but the connections you make. To make the right connections, you need the right image.

An Arts administrator (or department chairman, head of a reading series, editor of a magazine, manager of a bookstore, the head of distribution) cannot attract further funding if he has a controversial artist performing down the road at Potsawamie High. The administrator might even admire the teaching and writing of that artist, but he knows he has to ferret him out because he's not good for business.

The line for what was controversial got thinner and thinner. A poet might legitimately be drummed out of a program, as happened in Massachusetts, for screaming "Fuck!" over and over at a group of third graders (ostensibly to prove that words were only words and could be defused by repeating them often enough). But a poet could also quietly be waltzed out of a program for asking a teacher not to read the newspaper in front of the class while the poet was conducting a workshop, as happened in Pennsylvania. If the teacher happened to be the relative of a high-ranking state official, that official could get on the phone with the state arts council and state politicians and list dozens of infractions the poet had perpetrated, even though just a year before the official's relative had written an assessment of this same poet recommending that he return to her fifth graders.

The year was 1978. The poet was canned by the literature panel of the Pennsylvania Arts Council in a note that went, "It is generally not the policy of the Council to employ artists from out of state." However, the National Endowment for the Arts wrote the poet, "Where federal monies are involved, local arts councils cannot disqualify an artist on the grounds of geographical location." But when the NEA sent two representatives to Harrisburg to investigate the matter, they concluded: "We have spent the entire day investigating the files of the Pennsylvania Council on the Arts and can find nothing out of the ordinary in regard to their handling of their situation with your employment."

Enter Texas Senator Lloyd Bentsen who requested a meeting with NEA and claims in a letter that two phone calls and a note went unanswered. A number of now-prominent poets worked at that time in Pennsylvania Poets-in-the-Schools. None questioned their employer's decision, though they had worked with the poet for three years, drank beer with him, shared meals in his own home.

Such an example of injustice and betrayal is typical. Although I've used the Poets-in-the-Schools programs as an example, it illustrates the dominant ethic among artists all during this period: Stay cool, don't get involved; if another poet gets his ass in a sling, that's his problem.

All during my travels, I heard similar stories like the one involving Pennsylvania. I never heard a story of artists banning together to protect or at least get a fair hearing for one of their fellow artists when an institution decided to yank him around.

When I first went to Texas to work in a Poets-in-the-Schools program, an artist told me, "These programs are always in chaos. The only attitude you can take is what another painter told me: 'Just get the money and run.' Hassles won't get you anywhere."

Given the above, it is no accident that one of the two poets summoned to defend NEA before its critics on the National Council on the Arts in 1990 was Ed Hirsch, who railed at Joseph Epstein's suggestion that Hirsch and his like were "pampered."

So I find it ironic that so many writers are stepping forth now to defend the NEA, like children stripped of their favorite playground when all along they have never viewed the institutions that sponsored them as their institutions but as a benevolent daddy who had come along to help them at the right time. If the Poets-in-the-Schools programs did not work out, they could always hope to get a prize for a book, take up a new and perhaps less vulnerable sanctuary as a writer-in-residence at some college, or if luck was with them, on the tenure track in some MFA program. That so few artists have seen these institutions—publicly funded arts programs as well as universities, journals, bookstores, indeed the very streets, as *theirs*, explains why Robert Penn Warren

115

could say, in response to a *Life* magazine reporter's question, "There's a lot of talent out there but not much fire."

How can you have any fire in your writing when you are unwilling to respond to the oppressiveness of your own institutions, let alone the chronic waste and injustice of a theoretical democracy? To have any fire in your writing, or your life, would be bad for business. Jesse Helms is in the business of playing up to his constituents and getting re-elected. As with most other matters, there are no principles at stake in the Congress. It is expediency. Just as it is expediency that governs the thinking of all those writers signing petitions on behalf of the life of the National Endowment for the Arts. It seems the moral thing to do, and none of the biggies want to be thought slack on a matter which could diminish their considerable constituencies.

Where were Susan Sontag and Arthur Miller and E. L. Doctorow and all the rest when the chain bookstores began telling smaller publishers that they had to do a million dollars worth of business with them each year before such stores would buy and stock their books without going through a (profit-killing) distributor or other middleman.?

In the last 15 years, hundreds of independent bookstores have been driven out of business by high rents caused by artificially inflated real estate prices. Did the owners of such stores get any protection from writers, though it was precisely this type of bookstore that kept literature alive?

Most writers older than 45 got their impetus to write because they could accumulate a library out of 95 cent and $1.95 paperbacks. Now, these same books come in $10 to $14 trade paperbacks. Are those established writers going to go to bat in some way so a poor young person can buy their books and bring a new generation of readers into our society?

The National Writers Union reports that each week more and more grievances from writers pile up on its desks. Are all the signers of all the petitions hooting for the survival of NEA going to lend their expertise and the weight of their reputations to aid this organization in defense of writers getting cheated on contracts with publishers?

PEN regularly tries to bail some incarcerated foreign writer named Puck Wow out of difficulty; this is fine, but have you ever heard of them going to the defense of an American writer, even though censorship is more prevalent in this country than almost any other industrialized society? Try to write PEN: They will refer you to the Writers Union, to which only a few of their own members belong.

On the subject of such injustices, I had a brief run-in with Nadine Gordimer nine years ago, ironically at a conference in Mexico City entitled, "The Languages of Colonialism." I heard Nadine say to the packed auditorium, "I want my writing to speak for those who are voiceless." I later asked her how the "voiceless" would ever read her when Penguin was selling her books for the equivalent of $1, U.S., a lot of money across the border. I also asked her why she couldn't ask the sponsors of the event to bus in some interested students from the poor barrios of Mexico City if she was so concerned about those voiceless people she claimed to be writing for.

"What you need, young fellow," she said, (damned if I'm young!) "is a writers' cooperative. Something like Writers and Readers."

I always thought it was in the best interests of writers to cooperate, that it was instinctive and natural to cooperate. I feel like Seymour Krim (quoted in Poets & Writers by Gerald Nicosia) when he said, "Why can't writers just talk to one another as people? Why do they always shy away from talking about the things that matter in their work? It's foolish to be bitter becasue your talent is not as big as someone else's."

Krim is right. Writers aren't talking about the things that matter, not in their books, not in their workshops, not in their endless conferences. For the last twenty-five years what I've observed is competition, a lot in the writers under 50, a little less in the writers over 50.

Precisely because they treat it as a game, they are vulnerable to attack from without, fragile to the point of hysteria, as witnessed by the current debacle of their threatened institution, the NEA. But it was not until it was threatened from without that writers have treated NEA as their institution.

In bits and pieces, reviewers and critics such as Robert Peters, Jonathan Yardley, Lewis Lapham, Hayden Carruth and Richard Kostelanetz have been fussing over the mediocrity in U.S. writing for the last 15 years. But it wasn't till Tom Wolfe rang the church bells of alarm in Harpers' magazine in 1990 that writers got upset. Here was a best-selling author attacking them in a national journal. Much like severed ethnic groups in the Balkans, writers could only find unity in what they perceived as the oppressor outside their nationalistic boundaries. As Vanilla Tom went across the U.S. holdilng town meetings (usually for a handsome fee), writers showed up in vast herds, willing to pay $10 to $20, not to hear him, not to discuss the issues he had raised, but to register in quavering voices their disapproval that he would have the audacity to lump them all under the word "anemic."

1980 was the year of literature's Watergate, some masterful shenanigans in the awarding of individual grants that was generally labeled "cronyism." It was more like theft, and it was investigated by Hillary Masters and finally published (in edited form) in the *George Review* after being rejected by 17 other magazines. Outrage abounded; it was a legitimate public scandal. Yet, heaven help our stale metaphors if we have any public discussion of the so-called "poetry mafia". The arts, especially literature, are a reminder of the purity of our essential beings and must be kept hush-hush lest they be examined like the other breakdowns in our society.

This from of schizophrenia is no exception. The real master of it is Lewis Lapham, editor of *Harper's*, who has written what I consider to be the best essay on the state of U.S. writing. It's called "The Audible Silence" and was published in a literary quarterly whose identity I couldn't decipher from the Xerox copy Lapham mailed to me. "Given the brilliance of this article," I wrote to him, "and your connections in the media, why didn't you publish this in a more conspicuous journal?"

Lapham wrote back, "My friends told me that if I tried to publish this, I could put my career in a bottle and cast it in the wine-dark sea." With no apologies to Homer, Lapham, like a whole lot of others, is going to have it both ways. From time to time they'll poke at the system, but not so much and not in a way that could jeopardize their comfortable careers. Do not their "careers" summarize the lack of real examination we've had of a country in crisis?

Given an entire nation of careerists, is it any wonder language is now inflated to the point it hardly has any meaning? The repercussions of all this horse shit by these "professionals" are to isolate those writers who could really make a difference, who believe literature is not just a parlor game but the very conscience of a nation.

One such man who's been isolated because he does not play the game is Robert Peters. For 30 years Peters has been producing strong poetry, criticism and drama. But he would offer that most traitorous of ideas: You can never tell where you'll find truly vital writing.

This single idea usurps the whole daisy chain of isntitutional thinking. It is unforgivably populist. It throws "taste" to the four winds with the money crowd which is the only crowd that can now afford art. Most of all, Peters is unforgivably himself, free of cant and preconceptions; as such, he is an ugly threat to the current epidemic of digested fear and smug cautiousness.

The NEA has acknowledged Peters with a grant but it doesn't make any difference. The NEA literature section long ago fell into the trap of seeing writing as a means and not an end in itself; writers must see the NEA, and any other institution which affects writing, as their rightful home and not a sugar daddy for tough times. In short, for the NEA to have any meaning, there would have to be a revolution in the thinking of the people it benefits. Then, the NEA and its congressional backers would have to come to the understanding that "the first rule for any artist," as Brendan Behan said, "is to be against government."

I doubt that either of the two responsibilities will come to pass. As with a houseful of bedding filled with smallpox, the only way to rid the house of infection is to drag the bedding outside and set it on fire. A lot of sociologists and economists are predicting that social justice will soon come about through some cataclysm they can't name. Writers can't name it either but like so many of the "experts," they are restless for this change. They may be shocked to discover the change has nothing to do with words, that it is too late for words. In the words of Jean Giono, (a writer nobody reads), "People think only of adding to their comfort, heedless that one day true men will come up from the river and down from the mountain, more implacable and more bitter than the grass of the apocalypse."

field notes from a cuban jail:
on b. traven

The writer B. Traven went right to the Center of Hell and walked out the other side with a gold crown on his head and a smile on his face. B. Traven is the King of Writers, for this century and for most other centuries. He wrote deftly and quietly with none of the bombast that periodically sneaks into the works of Miller and Bukowski; there is not a hint of the literary mannerism that dominates the so-called classics that are taught in the world's classrooms. He writes from the comparative isolation of villages, mountains, jungles, ships at sea about people who do not have passports, social security cards, or any kind of identifying papers. According to the authorities these people do not exist, have never existed, yet most of our comforts—our teacups and our teabags, our tennis shoes and our stereos—are made by these Faceless of the Earth whose Hell if we bothered to think about it would make us vomit our croissants and decaffeinated coffee. The Twentieth Century is one vast shithole, unremitting and pissing on us by the hour. Traven was there; he sang and fought and danced in its flames. And when we are finished with a Traven book, we look up at the sky and we say, "Thanks, dear Sun God, for allowing me to breathe one more day."

For Traven not only documented the tortures of the damned, he showed us how to persevere with grace, with laughter, with a terrible strength that if we bothered to utilize it, every precinct captain from Fairbanks to Tierra del Fuego would quake in his patent-leather boots and sneak out the backdoor to his sheepfarm. Traven's heroes and heroines suffer every physical deprivation, every grief, every possible insult to their dignity and yet I always feel strong and complete when I finish a Traven book. Like all real writers, Traven alerts us to the fact that we create our lives, not some boss, not the government, not some company, not some regal institution in Oshkosh, Wisconsin or San Jose, Costa Rica. Us and us alone. In the middle of nowhere. Where civilization as we know it barely reaches.

His heroes and heroines are intensely practical; only in the case of a couple of village school teachers do they have much formal education; though they have been touched by the drift of socialist ideology so prevalent in the first thirty years of this century, they belong to no party and adhere to no ideology. His white heroes, like Traven himself, have strayed far from their origins and are perpetual students of nature, of primitive civilizations, and the effect of civilization on these primitive holdings near the jungle or in the mountains. Though Traven wrote from 1920 to 1968, what he does is recreate the first conflicts between the white man and the Indian; if the white men are alone they tend to respect the world of the mestizo and the Indian; if they are on vacation or represent a company, they view the brown-skinned man and woman as primitives who stand in the way of the white man's fortune. In the last seven books that he wrote, Traven increasingly takes on the point of view of the Indians of Southern Mexico, and the real miracle of the man who was B. Traven is born in these books.

For what finally emerges is a rebirth of certain words that have had the sauce wrung from them till they are dry pods. I am thinking of words like dignity, friendship, community, love, eternity, devotion, and freedom. Political sects and organized religions have got a hold of those words and used them as fronts to bully us and cow us and make us sit in the front row with our heads down, ashamed we were born, crying out internally for Jesus or Ronald or Dear Joseph Stalin or Reconstructivism or Mao-Tse-Tung or a new compact disc player to take our dreary souls and toss them away and outfit us with a new allegiance so that we are not so lonely, so that we might feel we after all belong somewhere. A Traven hero is very happy to be alive; life begins there, it begins with an allegiance to the dawn, a song, a personal prayer, a poem the way all Indians used to do when they stood at the door of their hut or teepee which always faced East. In other words life must begin each day with a sense of humility. It must begin with the notion that human beings—if that word is to have any meaning—are a part of a large and amazing creation, of which man is surely not the centerpiece. This was the foundation of the Traven philosophy and it flies in the face of everything we have been taught.

Traven was a moralizer and a teacher, generally two occupations which will put us to sleep in a hurry. But he wove his vision with such patience in a framework of leisurely storytelling with such attentiveness to detail and tone that we follow him with complete trust. There is that thing in Traven that no amount of rational thinking or literary criticism can account for: that is the 6th sense that every sentiment, every detail has been earned. And this happens because I don't think Traven was ever worried about being a writer; he no doubt had concerns that his writing would pull in enough to feed him but I'm sure he felt he would survive somehow, some way.

No, I think what really concerned Traven was the

question that no one I meet wants to talk about, that no one I meet wants to think about, that few writers or artists ever consider in their creations: how to be a man (or a woman) without being a bully? Or put another way, can we gain our food and lodging and sense of self-importance without enslaving others? Every ounce of Traven is addressed to this question at all times. And what if 99% of the people we meet or are going to meet in our lifetime have been so used to one form or another of slavery that it makes it impossible to treat them as free and equal persons? How to break this vicious chain of coerce or be coerced? It is this that turns us into dead men long before we are dead, that keeps us from enjoying life in our brief time on this earth. Each upheaval, each revolution, each turn in social, cultural, or political fashion has only put a new bully on the block, and each time people's subservience has become more pronounced. One hundred and ten years ago, a brilliant thinker in the fertile and lugubrious Russian mold named Vissarion Belinsky wrote, "What good does freedom do me if my neighbor is in chains?" "In each person there is a free soul and a slave and they fight for domination," wrote Maxim Gorky 30 years later.

Celine wasn't so generous. On this planet, he wrote, "one can lie or die." Celine wrote this in 1935 from Paris after prolonged visits to Africa and the United States. Traven, on the other hand, had the luck of a unique time and a highly original place. He arrived from Germany via China in Tampico, Mexico, in 1924; more important, within two years he would find himself in Chiapas, Mexico, one of the most unique areas in the world then and now. For it was only four years ago that Chiapas exploded across the world's newspapers and magazines because of a rebellion among various offshoots of the Tsotsil Indians—the very Indians that Traven wrote about—that expanded into an expression of many Mexicans the desire for a new ruling party. The implications reached far beyond Mexico and the Mexican stock market in which U.S., Canadian, and European investors have pumped more than a billion dollars during the past 15 years. At stake was the whole Indian slave system of Latin America where a tiny elite govern much the way they did 80 years ago. The Mexican stock market could not be allowed to collapse; not when Mexican workers would assemble televisions and stereo systems for eight or ten dollars a day and lordly investors could smile from their armchairs in Frankfort, Tokyo, and New York at the lordly dividends rolling in. Thus, President Clinton could commit millions of dollars to keep the Mexican Bolsa from collapsing. The teacups and electric dildoes of the investors' mistresses were at stake.

As men from the world's financial institutions met at mahogany tables to see what could be done, CNN was interviewing students in Chiapas. These students were holding aloft two books, Eduardo Galeano's *Open Veins of Latin America* and B. Traven's *Rebellion of the Hanged*. You would have thought such exposure would send a few book buyers to the store to check out Traven. But no such thing happened; the audience of intelligent people for an unusual author remained and remains hopelessly comfortable, hopelessly bored, hopelessly passive. I am writing this from a country in Latin America which attracts several thousand tourists each week from all the developed countries. For the last month I've been asking these tourists—many of them quite well-read—if the name B. Traven means anything to them? With all of them I get a shake of the head until I mention *The Treasure of the Sierra Madre* and then I get a smile of recognition.

on b. traven

At any rate, Chiapas had come full circle since the time of Traven. What he discovered there in 1924 was that the Mexican Revolution had just terminated. All of Mexico buzzed with a new belief in justice; workers organized; schools were built; the church was relegated to the back burner in the reorganization of this new society. This was also the period when the U.S. corporations and the U.S. government had its nose in every banana republic and was installing dictators who would make sure the fruit cocktail on American tables was picked by illiterates who were compensated with just enough money to survive. In Mexico, the U.S. oil companies were traipsing through every Eastern pueblo looking for gold, looking for oil, looking for anything cheap to buy so they could sell it for 500% profit in good old Oshkosh. Traven wrote about this in *The White Rose*, how an Indian chief is abducted by a U.S. oil company to get his land. But books have no power; they are nothing, paper to light the trash in the family incinerator. But a movie, a movie, ahh now we are talking. So when the Mexican film version of this book won all of the major Latin American awards in 1963, the U.S. State Department banned it from entering the United States. They did not think it important enough to ban Traven because no one was reading him anyway. It was around this year that Traven returned much of the advance monies to Alfred Knopf because a particular book did not sell even 3,000 copies.

But history has an odd way of coming back to piss on our dreams and our credit cards. In 1935, President Lazaro Cardenas nationalized many of the oil holdings and tossed out the American drillers. It was his son who in 1986 launched a series of candidacies around the platform of the completion of the 1910 Revolution that stirred the Lacandons and the Chamulas—Traven's old

william joyce

friends—who in turn began to rumble and made the bolsas tremble from Mexico City to Wall Street. History keeps coming at us and coming at us. Because what I am really talking about here—hoping somehow to reach you between your second croissant and your addiction to the *New York Times*—is nature. It is nature's nature not only to murder us in our sleep but to give and give and give, to shower us with all the delights of its startling womb—tasty fish, magnificent sunsets, shade to cool us, sun to heal our chests. It is in our nature—because we are nature too—to give but how many people do we know who can give, who have anything to give? People cannot give for the simple reason that they don't know how to take, take what nature has provided for them. They take the wrong things. When they don't get them, they start to push other people. They make ideas; they think these ideas will control people and make something they call "society" better. They build a building to put the ideas in. Then they hire the least intelligent but the most aggressive of their kind to guard the building lest anyone try to break in and steal the idea. It is all crazy. But then we are crazy—me, you, almost everything that we have built. We are not men, we are not women. We are things, even less animated than the furniture we buy; we are moved here, moved there. We think ourselves free, but on only a few occasions in my fifty years have I met a free man.

I met one the other day. I happened to be passing time in a Cuban jail. It seems I had slugged what I thought was a hotel worker who'd advised me the woman by my side was a prostitute and could not enter the hotel bar. Now let it be known that I am a great defender of women's rights. I will defend to my dying breath the right of any woman to sit on my head for $10.00 an hour.

To all of my seven ex-wives I paid four times that and the law had advised us we could "do it" legally. Well, it turned out that the hotel worker was really an undercover cop; I should have known because he spoke English with a Boston accent. They said I had broken his nose and that it would be weeks before his wife or his mistress would kiss him; I had disfigured him so badly.

The cops had their doubts; I am grey-haired and spindly and fifty; I don't look like a match for a strong wind. The Cuban cops kept going back to the room where the hotel worker-cop was being interviewed so they could peek under his bandages to ascertain that I had really done the damage I was purported to have done. They saw the stitches and the misshapen nose that no girl in her right mind would kiss and they returned to harangue me with "Capitalist Pig."

I fully admit to being a capitalist pig; that is why this essay took so long to get written to complete a book that nobody in their right mind would want to read. Why should I work for four weeks, 10 hours a day at a project that will never earn me a carton of Marlboro Lights when I can travel to the Cuban countryside, buy a 1953 or '54 Toppes Mickey Mantle baseball card for $48.00, fly to New York and sell it for several thousand dollars, return to Havana where I can hire three beautiful women for ten dollars an hour to take turns sitting on my face and singing the revolutionary songs from the Sierra Maestra days when a man was a man and sugar grew outside every palapa. You tell me. For these girls all have an uncle who took potshots at Meyer Lansky coming out of the Havana Hilton with a mulatta hooker on each arm and a bottle of Cutty Sark in his white tuxedo jacket. And when the girls get done biting my tonsils and mopping my floors, they sing the song, indeed the anthem of the old banana companies of United Fruit, "Yes, We Have No Bananas." We are all happy and the world of culture is not any worse for me not having written an overdue essay.

But what got me thinking about Traven and my debt to him was a very shabby man who gave me a pack of cigarettes while I was contemplating my navel in a Cuban jail. He was visiting a cousin who'd been arrested for selling blackmarket onions and he happened to notice the Mormon Tabernacle Choir of Cops singing, "Capitalist Pig." He handed me a pack of cigarettes, which by the way cost him the equivalent of two days wages, and said, "You need these worse than I do." This more than the police took the starch right out of me. All my pugilism melted and I thought, "Traven writes about just such people; perhaps it's my duty to talk about them." So the authorities were gracious enough to let me read Traven, largely because they could not locate my passport. I'd handed my bag with my passport to the insulted girl and she'd fled. Prostitution in Cuba has a sentence of four years in prison.

So, while a hundred policemen searched for the girl, another six policemen (Cuban intelligence) were plowing through every file, every computer printout for the identity of "William Stubbs," "Renaldo Hemingway," and finally, "William Joyce." Friends kept bringing the copies of Traven's books I had stored in my apartment so I was actually enjoying my new home, though the food was lousy and I sometimes had to read with the aid of a Zippo lighter. The only "William Joyce" who turned up on the computer weighed 225 pounds, was six-foot three inches, and was said to be promoting evangelical Baptist religion. I weigh 170 pounds, am 5 foot 11 inches and do not know the words to "Go Tell It on the Mountain."

Quirk of quirks, coincidence of coincidences. The

same thing that made me reread Traven was the exact cause for him writing in the first place—loss of any identifying papers.

Traven carried no papers because Germany put a death sentence on his head for treason. After World War I, Traven belonged to a group that wanted to organize a socialist state in a separatist Bavaria. Traven's closest associates were caught and executed. Traven got away; after hiding in various European countries, harassed and deported because he had no papers, he caught a ship from Antwerp to China, and from China he caught another ship for Mexico where he landed under an alias in 1924.

In his first novel *Death Ship,* in a passage that he later deleted from the book, Traven launches its principal theme that would later prepare him mentally to discover the world of the Indian. "The weaklings have always good police records and fine passports. And it is the weaklings and the cowards that make the criminals of the big cities. A strong heart knows how to struggle and he likes to struggle for his life." Traven lied about who he was and where he had been. The reading public, he said, was not entitled to a man's history nor his personality, only to his work. It was this denial and evasiveness about his background that ironically excited the reading public and the press. To date there have been more than forty books and 500 articles about "the real B. Traven" but not a single book about the value of his writing. In 1948, after the release of John Huston's *The Treasure of the Sierra Madre*, there were more than 300 European, American, and Mexican journalists running around Mexico looking for Traven, who had disguised himself as an innkeeper in Acapulco, Mexico. By this time, his books had been translated into 23 languages (from the original German, even though Traven usually tried to pass himself off as an American, writing in a butchered

English slang) and had sold millions of copies. But in the USA, a few thousand; and perhaps it is this mystery which should be talked about, not the abiding mystery of *"THE REAL B. TRAVEN."* Shirley Cloyes, director of the former publisher of Traven, Frederick Hill, says the poor sales are because of Traven's aversion to publicity. Fine, but does that explain his phenomenal sales in Europe where he had an almost equal lack of publicity? A separate book needs to be written on why U.S. reading audiences are so different from European and Latin American and Japanese readers. Then we would have some understanding why our grand republic remains so alone, so dominant and so isolated in world affairs. Part of the answer is that historically, other original writers have suffered the same neglect as Traven. I am thinking of Cossery (Egypt), Giono (France), Voinovich (Russia), Kohout and Hrabal (Czechoslovakia), Jules Renard (France), Elias Canetti (Bulgaria and Germany), Donoso (Chile), Carpentier (Cuba). These are huge, original talents that take your breath away and make you go back to them again and again. It's true that the American character is generous, especially toward underdogs; that is in our psyche and our history. But what that same character does with artists of any originality is abominable. It relishes inventors but cannot stand thinkers; like its step-sister England, it worships cleverness at the expense of any real profundity. Its geographical remoteness and horrid education system have made it disdain cultures different from itself. The United States is not alone in trying to exterminate its Indians, but it is alone in trying to cut their hair and shove an alien culture down their throats. For two centuries now we have thought we were the best, and at many things we were; but in the end we have proved ourselves the most divisive and the most lonely. An

American alone in a foreign capital is always a bit more lonely than a German or a Dane or an Argentinian. We have separated ourselves from the rest of the nations and we will pay a terrible price for it.

For example, in a famous short story called "Assembly Line" Traven dramatizes the relationship between Indian values and U.S. commercial rapaciousness; at the same time, he once and for all defines the relationship between the artist and an entire world ignorant of what goes into his art but desiring it nevertheless.

The Indian weaves baskets in amazing symphonies of color and design that reflect his love and interpretation of the natural world. Says Traven, "the most amazing thing was that these decorations were not painted on the baskets but were instead actually part of the baskets themselves. Bast and fibers dyed in dozens of different colors were so cleverly—one must actually say intrinsically—interwoven that those attractive designs appeared on the inner part of the basket as well as on the outside." Though each basket has woven in it, birds and antelopes, tigers and squirrels, and may take 40 to 60 hours to produce, the Indian artist made only the equivalent of pennies and was treated shabbily as he went door to door in this Mexican town selling his wares. Traven puts it all in perspective when he says, "He (the Indian) had little knowledge of the outside world or he would have known that what happened to him was happening every hour of every day to every artist all over the world. That knowledge would perhaps have made him very proud, because he would have realized he belonged to the little army which is the salt of the earth and which keeps culture, urbanity, and beauty for their own sake from passing away." Perhaps Traven is being ironic about culture and urbanity. At any rate, the Indian gets a visitor—Mr. E. L. Winthrop, fresh from a Rotarian convention in Hot Springs, Arkansas. E. L. goes ghaa-gaa over the sight of the little baskets; right away he sees them as an explosive best-seller on the New York market with an Easter egg in every basket and chicks hatching all over the continent. Pregnant to the point of hysteria with his marketing idea, Winthrop flies to New York where he convinces a candy merchant to buy ten thousand baskets. Traven's description of the psychology of the candy merchant defines once and for all the mentality of the modern entrepreneur: "Never before had he seen anything like them (the baskets) for originality, prettiness, and good taste. He, however, avoided most carefully *showing any sign of enthusiasm* (italics mine), for which there would be time enough once he knew the price and whether he could get a whole load exclusively."

Here in a few words, Traven dissects a whole civilization. The confectioner is no barbarian; he fully recognizes quality when he sees it. But he's instinctively ready to pare his emotions; emotions are not good for business. Damned if he is going to display any enthusiasm; that might make him lose leverage. Leverage, my friends, is what modern society is all about. We can't show people how we feel because we might end up on the short end.

Eventually, feeling itself atrophies; we become ghosts, pushed this way and that, whichever way the market dictates. The beauty, intelligence, joy, wholeness we were born with is subdivided into lots, all for sale under conditions which have more to do with asphalt and little to do with clear eyes and a smile that reflects the power of the sun. In such a subdivided face, the teeth take over, not with the enthusiasm of eating and relishing the

134

nourishment provided by the earth and man's adaptive intelligence, but teeth that masticate, teeth that slash and grind at the fiber of soul and do so out of a sense of impotency to fill the vacuum in the subdivided face that can no longer see, no longer hear, no longer sing. Emotion is the binder for body, mind, and spirit. When it is pared away in the name of marketing, the face caves in on itself; the liver and spleen crackle like dry tinder. Soon, atomic fusion. Power for sure, but no creation; particles of molecules sub-divided like the earth itself for underground parking lots. The soul of man ready to buckle under to the next bully on the block for it can no longer resist. Subdivided, no body can heal, and without healing there can be no love. Not romantic love but the love as reflected in Traven's book, *The Bridge in the Jungle*, where the white, civilized narrator can say at the end of a funeral to bury a young Indian boy, "He is my boy, my little brother, my fellow man who could suffer as I can, who could laugh as I can, and who could die as I shall die some day."

There was not merely a gap between what we know as white civilization and Indian culture, there was a positive wall which can never be climbed unless the so-called educated Western man relinquishes his statuary Ego and walks into the Indian village naked and on Indian terms. For in 1926, as a guide for German archaeological teams, Traven entered such villages of the Chamulas and the Lacandons. Everything in his life had prepared him for their world. He wanted desperately to find a place and a people where the word community meant something. He found it and it is reflected in *Bridge* which is the centerpiece of his writing. In this book there come together all the themes mentioned in the earlier books: the greed of individuals, but more often the corporations and oil companies to the north of Mexico; the ingeniousness, playfulness and capacity for sorrow of these Mayan Indians; the words freedom and dignity and how they work together.

I would like to say a word about the latter and then leave Traven to rest. He is no James Joyce; he is simple and accessible. Go read him, my explanations are not important compared with his patient and wise art.

My last story is a little run-in I had with Traven's Indians and how experience taught me what Traven's books could not. It was 1985 and I was sitting as professor of a writing class of unusually perceptive and hungry students at John Jay College in New York City. And I was not getting through. I was sitting there reading to them from *The Bridge in the Jungle* and alternately trying to explain the phrase, "Con su permiso," and how it captured a way of life different from the one I and my students had been educated in. I wasn't doing a very good job; there are times words fail us when we most need them, when we most want to describe what is important to us:

"With your permission." It seems so polite, so innocuous, but for the next six weeks I was haunted by the phrase. I woke in the middle of the night thinking about it but my head got no clearer in trying to phrase what it meant. Then one morning my fifth wife got a call to be a movie star. She was to be in a film and the film was to be made in Mexico. I was invited to go along. I was still 500 miles from the home of Traven's injuns but I took a bus there and as I was climbing the steps to my hotel, a very young Indian boy bolted out of the doorway and started downward carrying a bicycle twice as big as he was. I should have been the one to stop and let him pass but he reacted much quicker than I did. He dropped the bike, jumped to the side, and said, "Con su permiso."

He was maybe 11 years old. Though my Spanish was poor, from reading Traven I knew to say, "Pase." He nodded with a bright smile and left me wiser than I'd been in a long time.

There is more at stake here than a phrase that indicates courtesy or Indian humility. Traven says about this phrase, "To them (the Indians) it was impossible to cut through the breath of a human without having his permission to do so." The space immediately around us is special, inviolable, private. This is not what we own; ownership means nothing; it is what we are that counts. What we are is unequivocally given its space and its privacy. We can stand—according to the Chamula—in Timboctu in rags or on Fifth Avenue in New York in a linen suit and no one can cross our immediate space without asking in a gentle voice, "Con su permiso." In fancier terms, first decreed by the French Revolution, it is called "the rights of the individual."

It also signals me that the Indian in southern Mexico knows we must live by laws higher than the individual as long as those laws do not jeopardize the worth of the individual. And that basic to our every breath is a sense of humility. This does not translate to abjectness as it might in Christian theology. It is the awareness as that awareness connects with every fiber of our being that we as humans are part of a much bigger scheme that includes all things animate, and the worm and the mosquito must be given their due.

It is not the individual versus community, as we are often taught in an eighth-grade civics class, but the individual who instinctively identifies with the needs of the community, especially during crisis periods. When an Indian mother's young son falls from a bridge—constructed without railings by the local American company drilling for oil—and drowns in the river, everyone, even the white narrator, participates in her grief: "Many of the women brought armfuls of flowers; others brought wreaths hastily made out of twigs and covered with gold and silver paper. They put the flowers and the wreaths aside so as to spare the Garcia woman the pain of thanking them." Thus this prolonged death scene in *The Bridge in the Jungle* becomes a great hymn for life as a group of poor people reach out for one another and lift the sorrow of the grieving mother into a candle light that hovers above the entire story. Traven concludes, "It seemed that an occasion such as the one I had witnessed was necessary if one wanted to see those people as they really were, to see not only the dirt and their rags, but, what was more, their hearts and souls, the only things in man which count. Radios, Fords, and speed records do not count at all; they are but garbage when it comes to the final balance sheet."

That word "human" has been blasted to a numbing cliche, but I can think of no other book which so beautifully and resonantly returns that word to its rightful place. I give the final word to Traven: "A trip to a Central American jungle to watch how Indians behave near a bridge won't make you see either the jungle or the bridge or the Indians if you believe that the civilization you were born into is the only one that counts. Go and look around with the idea that everything you learned in school and college is wrong."

a bibliographic note

Charles Bukowski wrote over 40 books encompassing stories, novels, and poetry. He had the reputation of a "wild man" for his depictions of drunks, whores, and crackpots that find their way to his Los Angeles apartments, but like most reputations, this one leaves out an important truth: Bukowski was liable to say anything at anytime.

In 1967, he first attracted a large following through his column, "Notes of a Dirty Old Man," written for the LA alternative *Open City*. His work has been translated into a dozen languages and he has the status of a rock star in Italy and Germany. A film, *Barfly*, was made in 1987 about an early part of his life.

Among the prose, my own favorites are *Ham on Rye*, *Factotum*, and *Post Office*; or among the poetry, I would suggest *Love Is a Dog From Hell* and *You Get So Alone at Times That It Just Makes Sense*. But all of Bukowski makes for reading you've never met before.

Books by Irving Stettner:

THUMBING DOWN TO THE RIVIERA
152 pages. With 8 full-color watercolors reproduced by the author. $11.45 (postage included).

BEGGARS IN PARADISE
190 pages. With 12 ink drawings.
$11.45 (postage included)

STROKER ANTHOLOGY 1974-1994
384 pages. Introduction by Irving Stettner and 21 page
selection of his prose and poetry.
$19.95 (postage included)

The volumes listed above are all available from Stroker
Press, 124 N. Main St. #3, Shavertown, PA 18708

ON HENRY MILLER AND THE WO HOP
MYSTERY
32 pages. Limited edition.
$12 (postage included). Roger Jackson, Publisher, 339
Brookside Drive, Ann Arbor, MI 48105

SELF-PORTRAIT, 12 Poems for the Road by Irving
Stettner.
$7, plus $2 postage. Sun Dog Press, 22058 Cumberland
Drive, Northville, MI 48167

The novels and stories of B.Traven go in and out of print
in various editions. Perhaps the most comprehensive
body of his work in English is contained in the Hill and
Wang hardcover series of some years ago of his "Jungle
Novels," as well as other works. Edward Dee, Inc.
(Chicaago, IL) also has reissued the works. Most public
and university libraries have at least some of his books.
Try to find them. Then read them.

William Joyce loves a good cigar, especially when he can smoke it in a crowded restaurant. He was born in Pittsburgh and now travels through Latin America. His other books, *First Born of an Ass* (novel), *The Recorder of Births and Deaths* (stories), *For Women Who Moan* (poems), and *Listen America, You Don't Even Own Your Name* (poems) can be found in most good cigar shops.